Advance praise for *Change Management: The People Side of Change*

"The 5 tenets boils down the reason companies need Change Management to its essence—to help people adopt, apply and embrace changes that deliver a desired outcome. Jeff and Tim have done it again by translating a topic that can be fuzzy and esoteric to a level of clarity and purpose. The new edition is a must read for anyone starting on a journey of change or as a refresher for those who regularly manage, sponsor or lead change in an organization."

> Derinda D. Ehrlich
> Vice President, Global Operational Excellence
> Avnet Inc.

"The 5 tenets of change management give us new insights into how to approach and lead change. They are the foundational elements that have propelled the vision and growth of the Change Management practice and discipline."

> Rachel Shafran
> Senior Change Manager

"A must read for all executives, managers and change practitioners. *Change Management: The People Side of Change* provides a practical and yet comprehensive explanation of change management and how to apply the given tenets to achieve the desired objectives of the change. Based on years of research, the guidance in this book illustrates why effective change management is more than a project team role: it is also the responsibility of every executive, manager and supervisor in the organization. I will distribute this book broadly throughout my organization."

> Michael Nestor
> VP and Head, Change Management
> Bayer

"Tim and Jeff continue to craft thoughtful, practical, and tested advice for leaders who live in a world of continuous change—in other words, for all of us. This new edition adds an important thread to the conversation about the people side of change management: we change for a purpose. Clarity of intent that creates a vision of the future state not only inspires and anchors the change effort, but makes the measures of success obvious. 'What would we have to observe as evidence that the change effort was successful?'"

Stephen Wehrenberg, Ph.D.
Director of Human Resources Strategy and Executive Development
United States Coast Guard
Founding Director and Past President
Association of Change Management Professionals (ACMP)

"This book represents comprehensive coverage of change management concepts—Individual Change Management, Organizational Change Management and Change Competency. It is packed with insights and practical advice that will immediately help all organizations—government or business—at any level. Instituting these concepts and organizational ideas—and in turn teaching them to others—we have seen an increase in individual morale and organizational productivity."

Darlene Meister
Director, Diversity & Organizational Change Management
United States House of Representatives

"This is a very pragmatic handbook—built from systematic research and the field of change management—and I would recommend it to MBA students as real world preparation and to all managers as a Bible for helping with the daily challenges of change management!"

Todd D Jick
Professor
Columbia Business School

Change Management

The People Side of Change

An introduction to change management from the editors of the Change Management Learning Center

www.change-management.com

Jeffrey M. Hiatt
Timothy J. Creasey

Prosci Learning Center Publications

© 2012 Prosci Inc. All rights reserved.

Second edition

Printed in the United States of America

Library of Congress Control Number: 2012953518

Hiatt, Jeffrey M.; Creasey, Timothy J.
    Change Management: The People Side of Change

    p.   cm.

    ISBN 978-1-930885-61-5 paperback

    1. Organizational change - Management 2. Project
    management 3. Psychology - Change. I. Title

    HD58.8   2003
    658.4'06--dc20

Prosci Inc.
Loveland, Colorado, USA

Cover design by John Hamilton Design

The paper used in this publication meets the requirements of the American National Standard for Permanence of Paper for Printed Library Materials Z39.49-1984.

Volume discounts and direct orders are available from Prosci Inc. by calling +1-970-203-9332 or by visiting www.change-management.com

The terms PROSCI®; ADKAR®; AWARENESS DESIRE KNOWLEDGE ABILITY REINFORCEMENT®; and PREPARING FOR CHANGE, MANAGING CHANGE, REINFORCING CHANGE™ are trademarks of Prosci Inc. These trademarks may not be used without the prior written permission of Prosci Inc.

Contents

Appendices

CHAPTER 1

Why change management?

The results and outcomes of workplace changes are intrinsically and inextricably tied to individual employees doing their jobs differently. A perfectly designed process that no one follows produces no improvement in performance. A perfectly designed technology that no one uses creates no additional value to the organization. Perfectly defined job roles that are not fulfilled by employees deliver no sustained results. Whether in the workplace, in your community or in government, the bridge between a quality solution and benefit realization is individuals embracing and adopting the change.

Change management enables employees to adopt a change so that business objectives are realized. It is the bridge between solutions and results, and is fundamentally about people and our collective role of transforming change into successful outcomes for our organizations.

But what does it mean to manage the people side of change and what exactly is change management? How does change management create successful change? To answer these questions, it is necessary to establish the foundational tenets for change management. This grounding in the reality of how change actually happens will enable a better understanding and more robust application of the tools and processes for managing the people side of change. Each of these tenets will build on the other, and together they form the basis for the *what* and *why* of change management.

To begin, we need to have an anchor point that you as a reader can agree with and that establishes a starting point for this discussion: *We change for a reason*. As simple as this sounds, an underlying principle for managing change is that a future state can be envisioned that is different than today, and we are changing to that future state to achieve a specific and desired outcome.

When we say we change for a reason, that does not mean that the reason for every change is the same, only that there is a specific reason or objective for a given change. The reasons for change are as varied as change itself: revenue growth, improved customer satisfaction, reduced costs, better product or service quality, reduced risk exposure, improved quality of life and so on. Projects and initiatives are undertaken not because they are fun and exciting, but because there is an opportunity present or a problem to solve; most importantly, a chance to improve performance in a meaningful way. A fundamental assumption of change is that something different is possible. This gives us our anchor point and the first tenet for change management:

Tenet #1: We change for a reason.

To establish the second tenet, consider what makes a change come to life and produce a desired outcome. Is it the new technology or processes? How about new tools or new organizational structures? While these are necessary components of change, their presence alone does not create the change we are looking to achieve. Change has only truly occurred when individuals in the organization begin working in new ways: displaying new behaviors, using new tools, adhering to new processes and adopting new values. Individual shifts in behavior are the cornerstone of change. When numerous individual shifts are taken together as a whole, the desired future state of the organization is achieved. This leads us to Tenet #2: *Organizational change requires individual change.*

It is easy to think about change from an organizational perspective: the optimization of business processes, a new enterprise resource planning (ERP) application, electronic medical records, new accounting systems, the release of a new software tool, the move to a new office complex, the installation of a new piece of equipment in the manufacturing process, the shift toward paperless operations. These are all examples of changes that organizations are undertaking to improve performance, capture an opportunity or resolve an issue. But each of these changes ultimately requires certain individuals in the organization to do their jobs differently.

This is not to say that new technologies, improved processes, better tools and new organizational designs are not enablers of change, as these are certainly essential building blocks. However, change ultimately results from people adopting new skills and demonstrating new capabilities; and, while this may seem like common sense, we often assume that change at an individual level will just happen. For example, it is easy for a project manager or business leader to make the following assumptions: If I build it, everyone will use it; If I build it, everyone will use it immediately; and, If I build it, everyone will use it effectively. If these assumptions were always true, then each change would yield the desired outcomes every time.

Reality is different. If you build it, some people will use it, but not necessarily everyone. Some may never embrace the change, finding workarounds or simply opting out. If you build it, it will take time for people to get on board. Some people may change quickly, while others may move very slowly. Finally, if you build it, each person will use it at a different level of proficiency, some very effectively and some very poorly. The realization of change, even large-scale organizational projects and initiatives, is, at its core, an individual phenomenon. In other words, the degree to which a change produces results is directly correlated with individual change, hence the second tenet:

Tenet #2: Organizational change requires individual change.

When you consider that the realization of a change and the achievement of specific outcomes is tied to people, we can ask the right questions: How many total employees will engage in the change versus how many will opt out or find work-arounds (referred to as the ultimate utilization of the change)? How quickly will our employees get on board with the change (the speed of adoption)? How effectively will the change be implemented at an individual level (proficiency)? Since change is ultimately an individual phenomenon, it is these individual factors that drive or constrain the value a change creates. This leads us to the third tenet: *Organizational outcomes are the collective result of individual change.*

Specifically, the closer you are to 100% engagement with employees (a 100% utilization rate), then the closer you are to achieving 100% of the desired outcomes. Likewise, the faster employees embrace the change, the sooner the benefits are realized. For proficiency, the skills or competency demonstrated by employees directly correlates to the degree the benefits can be achieved.

On the other hand, the closer these human factors are to zero percent, the more likely the change will be viewed as a failure and the objectives will go unmet. For example, if a solution to a problem was developed, but no one implemented or used the new solution, then the business objective failed, even if the technical solution was developed exactly to specifications. Equally problematic is a change that was intended to be implemented in three months that instead takes two years. Ultimate utilization, speed of adoption and proficiency are the human factors that impact the overall return on investment and the degree to which the desired outcomes are achieved. Success, specifically delivering results and outcomes, depends on individuals embracing and adopting the change.

For example, consider the deployment of a large ERP system in a manufacturing company. The system was end-to-end, connecting customer order entry directly to manufacturing and inventory control. The goal of the implementation was to accelerate the order fulfillment process for customers and increase inventory accuracy, while enabling just-in-time manufacturing. Tom, an order fulfillment specialist in the warehousing department, received a customer order through the new system. He knew he had the product because he had seen it in the warehouse earlier that day. However, when he attempted to process the order, the ERP system listed the current inventory as "0." Tom could not ship the product sitting right there on the shelf because the new process required that the item be present in the inventory module of the new ERP system. When the problem was investigated, it was determined that one individual in manufacturing was resistant to the change and was not entering new inventory into the system in a timely manner.

This example shows several of the tenets at work. First, the reason for this change was not the new ERP system. The reason for the change was faster customer service and more accurate inventory control. Second, failure to manage the people side of change in the manufacturing group resulted in a failed outcome for the customer, not just a delay in the implementation of the system or frustration on Tom's part. Third, implementing system and organizational changes did not, in and of itself, produce results. Only through individual change and the new capabilities of individual employees could they realize a new future state and the associated business outcomes. Finally, Tom changing by himself was not enough. The overall outcome for the organization was the collective result of many individual contributors. Each person in the process chain must embrace and engage in the change in order for the desired outcomes to be achieved.

When project managers and business leaders assume that the human factors of change (ultimate utilization, speed of adoption, and proficiency) will automatically reach 100% the moment a change is introduced (or at the "go-live" date), they fall into the trap that designing and implementing a business solution is sufficient to achieve results. Without the engagement of each employee who must do his or her job differently as a result of the change, we lack tangible benefits from change, hence the third tenet:

Tenet #3: Organizational outcomes are the collective result of individual change.

So if you are asked, "Why change management?" the answer is simple: to ensure that each change in our organization produces the results we are expecting. If you are then asked, "What is change management?" or "What is organizational change management?" the answer and the fourth tenet is: *Change management is an enabling framework for managing the people side of change.* The reality in organizations today is that employees have choice, capacity limitations and capability constraints. Change saturation is at an all-time high. Resistance to change from employees is the norm and not the exception, especially when change is being imposed by others. Failing to lead the people side of change results in lower utilization, slower speed of adoption and poorer proficiency; stated simply, it results in less benefit from the change.

For this reason change management should not be viewed as simply a mechanism to reduce employee resistance, or a plan to mitigate the risk of negative things happening to the organization during change. Change management provides an organizational framework that enables individuals to adopt new values, skills and behaviors so that business results are achieved. Change management is about engaging the passion and energy of employees around a common and shared vision, so that the change becomes an integral part of their work and behavior.

Change management, as a practical matter, leverages the normal mechanisms within an organization to influence and develop employees through broad activities, such as communications, training and visible sponsorship. At the same time, change management enables action at an individual employee level through coaching and resistance management. "Change managers" refers not just to project team members or change management practitioners. Change managers include organization leaders, executives, managers, front-line supervisors and employees; all of whom enable individuals within an organization to transition from their own current state to a new future state. All of these change management activities and roles comprise a discipline and field of study that enable individual and organizational transitions, hence the fourth tenet:

Tenet #4: Change management is an enabling framework for managing the people side of change.

This leads us to the fifth and final tenet: *We apply change management to realize the benefits and desired outcomes of change.* This concluding principle is an essential and distinguishing quality of change management. Unlike project management, which is focused on the realization of a technical solution, change management is focused on the achievement of the desired results or outcomes of the change by managing people through their own transitions. This tenet is supported by research. Prosci's benchmarking studies show that projects effectively applying change management were six times more likely to meet their project objectives.[1]

So while training, communications, sponsorship, resistance management and employee coaching are critical elements of change management, they do not define change management. In other words, we do not apply change management to enhance communications and training, or to implement employee recognition programs.

Nor do we apply change management only to reduce the risks to the organization during change, such as lower employee morale, productivity loss, undesired turnover or negative impacts on customers. While a strong case for change management can be made on mitigating risks, it is a classic case of "necessary but not sufficient." Change management has a more important and primary objective: to increase the probability that the future state is realized and that the associated outcomes (objectives of the change) are achieved. *Change management is the application of processes and tools to manage the people side of change from a current state to a new future state so that the desired results of the change (and expected return on investment) are achieved.* This leads to the fifth tenet:

Tenet #5: We apply change management to realize the benefits and desired outcomes of change.

These five tenets comprise the *what* and *why* of change management. They describe the universal truths about how change happens and why a discipline is needed that focuses on enabling individual change. These tenets also allow you to establish the value proposition for change management in your organization.

Summary

Change management is the application of processes and tools to manage the people side of change from a current state to a new future state so that the desired results of the change (and expected return on investment) are achieved.

Change management is necessary because:

1. **We change for a reason.**

2. **Organizational change requires individual change.**

3. **Organizational outcomes are the collective result of individual change.**

4. **Change management is an enabling framework for managing the people side of change.**

5. **We apply change management to realize the benefits and desired outcomes of change.**

The high-level conclusions you can draw from these tenets are simple yet will profoundly impact the approach you take to lead change.

We apply change management for one primary reason: to ensure that the desired results from the change are achieved.

To lead change at an organizational level, you must be able to lead change at an individual level. Change management is only effective when you combine the processes and tools for organizational change management with the processes and tools for individual change management.

Change management is not a one-person job (or the job of one team). The roles required to execute a change management plan include senior leaders, front-line supervisors, middle managers, specialists from HR and OD, employees and designated resources on a project team. Unlike project management, which is executed by a trained project manager, change management is architected by change management professionals but executed by many players in an organization, from top-level executives to front-line supervisors.

Finally, we measure the success of change management by measuring the degree to which the objectives of the change are realized.

References

1.   Prosci. (2012). *Best Practices in Change Management.* Loveland, Colorado: Prosci Learning Center Publications.

CHAPTER 2

Change concepts

Change management is the application of many different ideas from the fields of business, organizational development and psychology. As changes in organizations have become more frequent and necessary for survival, the body of knowledge known as "change management," including change leadership, has also grown to encompass more skills and knowledge from each of these fields of study. While this may be a good trend overall, the result is often too many models and too much confusion.

Most change management models in use today are in the form of a process or set of steps. These processes or activity lists were developed through trial and error, and are based on experiences of experts in the field of change management. In some cases these experts have created a standard process based on their consultancy models. These experts often use the same processes with their clients that are published in their books, articles and training materials.

Unfortunately, the underlying lessons and concepts that resulted in these change management processes are not always clear. In many cases the concepts are not even discussed as part of the resulting model. In a sense, what you learn is the *how* but not the *why*. The years of practical experience and knowledge that form the basis for these processes are not readily available to business managers.

A story about a young man watching his mother prepare a roast illustrates the importance of this point. Each time his mother cooks a pot roast, she cuts two inches off each end of the roast.

The son asked, "Mom, why do you cut the ends off?"

"I don't know," replied Mom, "that is the way Grandma always did it."

The son decided to investigate with a series of phone calls, first to Grandma, then to Great Grandma. Grandma said she did it just the way Great Grandma showed her. After talking with Great Grandma, the son discovered that she cut the ends off the roast because her oven and cooking pan were too small, and she had to cut the ends off to make it fit.

Mom and Grandma knew the *how* – cutting two inches off each side of the roast – but not the *why* – because the original pan was too small. Ovens and pans are larger now and it is no longer necessary to shorten the roast.

Understanding the *why* makes you better at doing the *how*. Change management is not a matter of simply following steps or applying tools. Since no two changes are alike, following a recipe for change management is not enough. The right approach will be specific to the situation. If you do not understand the *why*, changes can fail even when standard processes are followed.

Research with hundreds of project teams has shown that a one-size-fits-all approach is not sufficient. To be effective at leading change, you will need to customize and scale your change management efforts based on the unique characteristics of the change and the attributes of the impacted organization.

To accomplish this customization, an understanding of the psychology of change and key guiding principles is vital. You will then be able to work with many change management methodologies and adjust your approach according to the size and nature of the change, ultimately making your change a success.

Core concepts for change management

The central concepts that will impact your change management activities are shown in Figure 1. The overview of concepts and ideas presented here is not intended to be an in-depth psychological analysis. Rather, the focus will be on the key insights from these concepts that impact the effective application of change management.

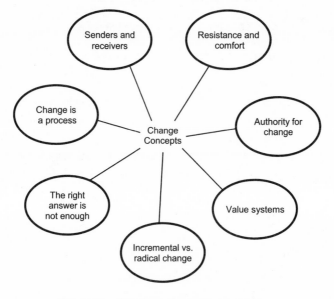

Figure 1 - Primary change concepts

Concept 1 - Senders and receivers

Every change can be viewed from the perspective of a sender and a receiver. A *sender* is anyone providing information about the change. A *receiver* is anyone being given information about the change.

Senders and receivers are often not in a *dialogue* at the onset of a change. They can talk right past one another as a sender focuses on the business issues and the receiver processes the personal implications (see Figure 2). What a sender says and what a receiver hears are often two very different messages.

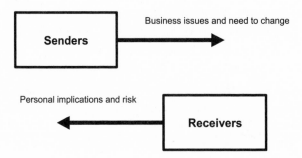

Figure 2 - Sender and receiver disconnect

For example, if a supervisor sits down with an employee to discuss a major restructuring project within the company, the supervisor may be enthusiastic and positive. She may cover all the key messages including the business reasons for change, the risk of not changing and the urgency to change for the organization to remain competitive. The supervisor may even emphasize that this is a challenging and exciting time. However, when the employee discusses this change at home over dinner, the key messages to his family are often:

"I may not have a job."

"The company is having trouble."

The supervisor may spend 95% of the conversation talking about the business and 5% talking about the implications to the employee. At home, the employee is more likely to spend 95% of the time talking about the impact on him personally and 5% on the issues facing the company.

The consequence is that much of the key business information communicated by the supervisor to the employee in this first conversation is not heard. It is overshadowed by concerns related to job security and fear about change.

Many factors influence what an employee hears and how that information is interpreted. Examples of these factors include:

- Their other career or educational plans

- Their situations at home or with personal relationships

- Their past experience with other changes at work

- What they have heard from their friends or work colleagues

- Their current performance on the job

- Whether or not they trust or respect the sender

Now multiply these factors by the number of employees who are the receivers of change messages and the number of managers who are the senders of these messages. You can begin to appreciate the challenge faced by many businesses as they communicate change to their employees.

Preferred senders

Based on Prosci's change management research report with 650 participants,[1] employees prefer two primary senders of change messages. Not surprisingly, they also prefer specific message content from each of these senders. Immediate supervisors are the preferred senders of messages related to personal impact including:

- How does this impact me?

- How does this impact our group?

- How will this change my day-to-day responsibilities?

When it comes to personal issues, receivers want to hear from someone they know and work with regularly, namely their supervisor.

CEOs or executive leaders are the preferred senders of messages related to business issues and opportunities including:

- What are the business reasons for this change?

- How does this change align with our vision and strategy?

- What are the risks if we do not change?

When it comes to business issues and why the change is needed, receivers want to hear from the person in charge.

The sender and receiver concept is very relevant to the actions taken by change management teams, project teams and business leaders in the change management process. Typically, executives, project teams and supervisors are the *senders* of key messages. They follow a prescribed communications plan to share information about the change. These communication activities are part of organizational change management.

In some cases, however, managers do not assess what their employees actually heard, nor do they understand how that information was processed. They merely complete a communication activity, check off a box, and move on to the next activity. A poor assumption is that *"employees heard just what I said and understood exactly what I meant."*

More likely, employees heard only a fraction of what was said, and their translation of that message will be unique to their personal situations. Some employees may have heard more than what was said, or will make up answers to questions that they do not understand. The answers they make up are typically worse than reality.

Realizing that *what receivers hear and what senders say are not always the same* is the first step to understanding that change management cannot be reduced to a set of activities or steps. Managers must not only be clear in their communications, they must also *listen* to employees to understand how their messages are being received. Change management communication is only effective when employees have internalized the change messages and can begin the transition process.

Concept 2 - Resistance and comfort

A common mistake made by many business leaders is to assume that by building awareness of the need for change, they have also created a desire among employees to engage in that change. The assumption is that one automatically follows the other. Some managers fall into the trap: If I design a "really good" solution to a business problem, my employees will naturally embrace that solution. Resistance from employees takes these managers by surprise and they find themselves unprepared to manage that resistance.

So why do employees resist change? From personal experience, we all know that change creates anxiety. The current state has tremendous holding power, and the possibility of losing what we have grown accustomed to (and comfortable with) creates worry and uncertainty. The future state of workplace changes is often unknown or ill-defined, and this creates fear about what lies ahead.

Anxiety and fear are powerful emotions that by themselves create resistance to change. But there is more to resistance than our emotional response. We must examine the other drivers that influence an employee's resistance to change. From a work perspective, were employees involved with designing the change and do they know why the change is being made? Or, were they taken by surprise by the change? Do they believe that the reasons for making the change are valid and do they trust the "senders" of the change message? From a personal perspective, how might the change impact them?

When employees consider how a change will impact their personal situation, they will include all aspects of their life including family status, mobility (are they in a position to be flexible in terms of where they live?), financial security, age, health, career aspirations (are they where they expected to be at this point in their life?), relationships at home and at work, educational background, upcoming personal events and past success in this work environment (promotions, recognition, compensation).

For example, a person's financial situation or health may cause them to make choices related to a change that, on the surface, do not appear logical, and may look like resistance to the change. Only when you look beyond the symptomatic resistance can you see the underlying personal reasons for their behavior.

To make this personal angle a bit more complex, we should also recognize that an employee's internal value system and "view of self" also contribute to whether or not he or she will resist a particular change. Without exploring the psychology of human behavior in depth here, we cannot understand that what motivates a person is unique to that person. We each "march to a different drummer," and a given change may or may not align with where we envision ourselves in the future. Each of us also has an innate ability to assess whether or not we could be successful in the "future state" should we decide to move forward. This "probability of success" plays yet another role in our decision to support or to resist a change.

Now add the environment or context within which the change is occurring. Employees will consider the organization's success of past changes, how much change is already going on, and the reinforcements or rewards that were part of past changes. In short, the organization's culture and history directly impact a person's resistance to new changes. If a company has a history of starting changes and not following through, or if it has a track record of allowing some groups to opt out of a change, then these past events weigh heavily on the willingness of an employee to engage in a new change.

You can begin to appreciate why resistance to change is a normal and natural reaction to change. Add together the emotional response, an individual's personal situation, and the organization's culture and history with change, and you have a potentially volatile mixture that can drive resistance. The question, therefore, is not *if* we will encounter resistance to change, but rather *how* we support our employees through the change process and manage that resistance.

We must, at some point, ask the question: How much resistance might we avoid if we would apply change management early and effectively? In the example with the ERP implementation case study, rather than simply designing a "great" solution to the manufacturing and inventory structure and beginning implementation, a proactive change management program could have been put in place to engage and support employees through the transition. Rather than waiting for resistance to happen, or being taken by surprise when key employees resisted the change, the leadership and project team could have assumed that resistance to change is normal and natural. If they had started with this as a basic presumption of change, then their actions and planning could have prevented the project failure and unfortunate consequence to the customer.

Concept 3 - Authority for change

When we think of change, we often think of leaders. Some person or group is the guiding authority that determines and enables change to occur. The notion that we need people to set direction, solve problems, create a vision and lead us to a better future is part of our heritage. It is present in families, communities, companies and government.

Not surprisingly, the number one success factor for managing change from the research is visible and active executive sponsorship or change leadership.[2] This factor alone has been cited in studies more frequently than any other requirement for effective implementation of change.

In the common language of change management, the leader has the name sponsor or primary sponsor. Connor (*Managing at the Speed of Change*) defines sponsor as "the individual or group who has the power to sanction or legitimize change."[3] Using this definition, we can readily identify the leader(s) who can enable a specific change to happen. What is equally important is what these leaders do: What defines change leadership or *sponsorship*? Prosci's research over a 14-year period identifies three roles that define sponsorship during change:[4]

- Sponsors actively and visibly participate in the change.

- Sponsors build a coalition of sponsorship between key business leaders.

- Sponsors communicate directly with employees about why the change is needed.

When these roles are carried out effectively by a leader of a change, several things can be observed. First, sufficient resources and funding are available and priorities are established between competing initiatives. Roadblocks are removed and the sponsor stays active throughout the entire project. Second, other senior leaders sponsor the change in their areas and manage resistance as necessary. A coalition of sponsorship is formed that leads and supports the change. Finally, employees understand why the change is being made and how the change aligns with the vision for the organization. If they have objections or resistance to the change, they have a productive channel through which they can resolve their objections.

On the other hand, when a change lacks sponsorship you will see confusion among competing changes and a lack of resources for the change. Managers and other leaders in the organization fail to sponsor the change in their areas, and resistance is not managed. Employees do not know why the change is happening nor do they understand the risks of not changing. The change languishes and fails to produce results.

While the criteria and roles for a sponsor may seem straightforward, many projects today struggle because they lack sponsorship for their change. In some cases executive sponsors authorize the change (sign the check) and kick off the project, and then disappear. They abdicate the role of sponsorship to a mid-level manager or consultant. In other cases the sponsor may be at the wrong level in the organization. They simply lack the power or control to implement the change. Equally problematic is a sponsor whose credibility is questioned by employees. Some employees will distrust the change sponsor, even if the sponsor holds a senior position, if past changes under the sponsor's leadership have failed or if employees lack respect for the sponsor.

A common mistake made by inexperienced project managers is not assessing if the change has sufficient sponsorship to succeed. Three possibilities for failure include:

- Not having the sponsor at the appropriate level in the organization, or

- Having the right level of sponsor but he or she lacks the ability to act as an effective sponsor, or

- Having the right level of sponsor but he or she lacks the desire to implement this change.

Moving forward with a project without the necessary sponsorship and change leadership will likely result in wasted resources, project delays and/or failure during implementation.

Concept 4 - Value systems

In the best-selling book, *Stewardship*,[5] Block describes the values that have been the centerpiece of traditional, hierarchical organizations: control, consistency and predictability. These values dictate that decision making is at the top of an organization, leaving the execution and implementation to the middle and bottom layers.

The belief system in this type of organization is more akin to a military structure. The predictable and desired reaction to a change is compliance with any new direction, and this behavior is encouraged and rewarded. For a leader in this type of organization, authority is typically not questioned. The value systems reinforce compliant behavior, and employees understand how they will be rewarded or punished. The values of control, consistency and predictability create an environment where change is simply a plan to implement or an adjustment to a mechanical system. Decision making is top-down.

Unfortunately, as Block clearly presents, many employees are unable to serve in the best interest of the customer in this traditional value system because they lack ownership and accountability. They do not have decision-making authority nor the required business knowledge to act on behalf of the customer.

Then value systems began to shift. Business improvement initiatives that empowered employees – including Edward Deming's teachings following World War II, the earliest quality circles from Toyota, Six Sigma from Motorola, Organization Development, Total Quality Management (TQM) from AT&T and Ford – came to the forefront. During this period, many businesses embraced one or more of these business improvement methods and the associated belief system. Over the course of implementing these improvement strategies, new values were imparted to employees, including empowerment, accountability and continuous improvement (looking for ways to improve what you do every day).

A new culture evolved within many businesses. Employees began to take ownership and responsibility for their work. They began striving to improve their work processes and overall performance. These new values have improved business productivity and the ability to react to customer needs. However, the evolution from the traditional values of control, predictability and consistency – values that made change relatively simple to implement – to the new values focused on accountability, ownership and empowerment has made the implementation of top-down business change more difficult.

The net result is that these same employees now question and resist new change initiatives. The response of the employee has shifted from "yes, sir" to "why are we doing that?" If your employees have embraced some or all of these new values, change management is not an option for successful change, it is a requirement. The values of

	Old Values	New Values
Command	**"Jump"**	**"Jump"**
Response	**"How high?"**	**"Why?"**

Figure 3 - A contrast in values

your organization and your culture create an overlay for everything we do. Recall that up to this point we have presented several core concepts around change: Communication is essential yet there is often a disconnect between senders and receivers; resistance is a normal human reaction to change; leaders bring authority and legitimize change within an organization. Overlaying each concept is the reality that the culture and values of an organization uniquely and tangibly impact how these concepts will play out for any given change.

For example, every individual has an intrinsic need to accept and acknowledge the benefits of a change (what's in it for me?) in order to fully support it. However, cultural factors influence whether that inquiry is approached from a collective or individualistic perspective. Some value systems focus on "what's in it for us as a group?" while others take great stock in "what's in it for me as an individual?"

A second example comes in the way resistance is displayed or expressed. In some organizational cultures, resistance is very visible. Employees readily make their objections known openly and loudly. In other cultures, particularly those with values around deference to authority, dissent is much less overt, often taking the form of passive or underground resistance. Resistance to change is universal; how an employee actually resists and what that resistance looks like will depend on culture and values.

Now add the globalization of our economies and the diverse workforce of today's organization, and you can recognize that not only does culture play a key role in how individuals respond to change, different cultures within an organization create a heterogeneous landscape in which change is implemented. The effect of these shifts in culture and values over the past 50 years is that change management is needed more today than ever before. Leaders must undertake change from a holistic perspective that addresses both the organization as a whole and the individual. Individual change management models are necessary, in parallel to organizational change management methodologies, to support employees who operate with modern value systems.

Concept 5 - Incremental versus radical change

Employees will react differently to a change that is incremental as compared to a change that introduces a dramatic shift to what they know – a radical change. The right approach and amount of change management required by a given project or initiative is unique and specific to the magnitude of the change, specifically how different the change is from the current state. Change can be broken down into two types as shown in Figure 4.

Type 1 – Incremental change: In this change environment, a change will take place over a long period of time.

The objectives of the change are small and deliberate. These types of changes are not normally driven by financial crisis or immediate demand for improvement, but rather a general focus on performance improvement.

Type 2 – Radical change: In this environment, immediate and dramatic change is required over a short time period. Often driven by a crisis or significant opportunity, these changes are meant to produce dramatic performance improvements in business processes, structure or systems. Example initiatives that create radical change include business process reengineering, regulatory changes, mergers and acquisitions.

Changes that are incremental in nature typically require less change management because you are asking your employees to make a smaller leap from what they

Incremental
Improvement
(TQM, Six Sigma)

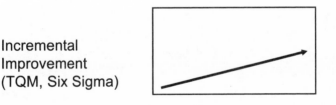

Radical
Improvement
(BPR, reengineering,
restructuring)

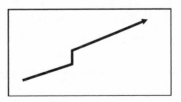

Figure 4 - Degrees of change

know and are comfortable with. Radical changes, on the other hand, require more change management. The future state is more uncertain than in incremental change, and the comfort of the status quo is left farther behind when we ultimately make the change.

Change management is most effective when it is flexible and scaled to fit the particular change at hand. No two changes will require exactly the same process or same level of change management. Even the activities and roles will change. Applying a "one-size-fits-all" approach is not effective. Change management must be scaled based on the characteristics of the change (how big it is and how many people are affected) as well as the attributes of the organization impacted by that change.

Concept 6 - The right answer is not enough

Isn't the "right" answer enough to secure buy-in from employees? Consider this typical evolution of events: There is a problem or opportunity identified in the organization. A team of the best and brightest is assembled to develop a solution. Countless hours and dollars are spent on crafting the right solution. When the project team has the right solution designed, it quickly moves to go live. The go-live date comes and the system or process is "turned on." Yet, instead of automatic compliance, there is rampant resistance. Employees find workarounds and some simply ignore the change. Although the project team arrived at the "right" answer, little or no improvement was achieved. Is this example the exception or the rule in your organization? Is not the right answer to a business problem enough?

Certainly it is important to come up with the right

solution to an issue or opportunity facing the organization. Project teams and consultants have experience and technical expertise in identifying what needs to change, evaluating different solution alternatives, selecting the right approach, and developing a solution to meet the technical requirements of the situation. Most of the time the team is able to create a solution that solves the technical issue or opportunity.

However, simply arriving at the "right" or "best" solution is not sufficient to ensure that performance is improved or results are achieved. Ultimately, changes come to life through the behaviors and work processes of individual employees. The right answer alone does not create buy-in. The right answer alone does not create commitment. The right answer alone does not mitigate resistance or eliminate fear.

Just having a solution that is technically "right" does not guarantee that employees will make the necessary changes to their behaviors and work processes. Employee commitment, buy-in and adoption do not stem from the rightness of the solution, but rather from employees moving through their own change process. It takes more than the right solution to move employees out of the current state that they know and into the future state they do not know (and sometimes fear).

Why is this principle, "The right answer is not enough," so important for change leaders? Many business leaders believe that if they can develop a great solution, there won't be resistance to change. To examine if this is a good assumption, consider the data around employee resistance from Prosci's 2012 *Best Practices in Change Management* benchmarking report. In rank order, the top reasons employees resist change are: 1) Lack of awareness of the need for change, 2) Impact on current job role,

3) Organization's past performance with change, 4) Lack of visible support from managers and 5) Job loss.[6]

None of the reasons identified by participants in this study are related to the rightness of the solution! The top reasons for resisting a change – for both employees and managers – are not related to whether or not the solution is correct. They are rooted in how an individual employee or manager understands and experiences the change process. If the top reasons for resisting a change are not related to whether or not the answer is correct, then simply coming up with the right answer is not enough to mitigate or eliminate resistance.

Take for instance, a new logistics process and application to expedite shipments to customers. While it is important to architect an effective platform and technical solution, the value of having a new system comes from the individuals who input data and use that data to make decisions. Without change management, a perfectly designed logistics application will sit unused, or even potentially misused. If employees in the warehousing area do not enter data about current inventory, then employees in the customer service group lack the information they need to communicate shipping status to customers. When one part of the chain breaks down, the entire process fails to operate effectively. In the end it is not about the rightness of the solution, but how well that solution has been embraced by employees. Before these employees can embrace a change, they need answers that have nothing to do with the rightness of the solution. Employees want answers to questions like:

- Why are we changing in the first place?

- What is wrong with how things are done today?

- Why is the change happening right now?

- Are senior leaders truly committed to this change?

All of these are real and ever-present questions that employees have in times of change, and none of them are related to having the "right" solution. The risk is that if a team only focuses on developing the right answer, they may ignore the people side of change and end up installing a change that delivers no benefit to the organization. Change management adds structure and intent for moving employees from their current state to their future state. Through effective communication, sponsorship, coaching, training and resistance management, employees are able to engage with and support a change. Change management provides a repeatable and rigorous approach to helping individuals move forward and adopt a change to their day-to-day work, which is what enables projects to ultimately deliver results.

Concept 7 - Change is a process

The concept of change as a process has been well documented in change management literature for many years, including early work by Bridges (*Transitions*)[7] and by Beckhard and Harris (*Organizational Transitions*).[8] By breaking change down into discrete time periods or states of change, leaders can adapt their strategies and techniques based on where they are in the change process (see Figure 5).

The most common lesson from this model for change is that we must avoid treating change as a single meeting or announcement. Change is not implemented in a single moment, and likewise, the role of business leaders in sponsoring change should not be reduced to a single event. The sponsor's role in change must be to be active and visible in all phases of the change process.

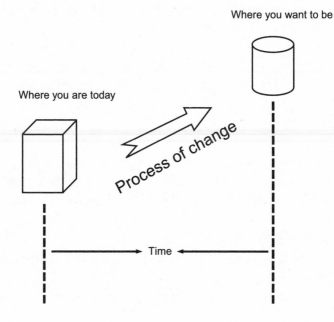

Figure 5 - The process of change

A larger lesson from the principle of *change is a process* is found when you examine how individuals navigate change. The Prosci® ADKAR® Model characterizes the process for individual change in five key steps:

- **Awareness** of the need to change

- **Desire** to participate in and support the change

- **Knowledge** about how to change

- **Ability** to implement new skills and behaviors

- **Reinforcement** to keep the change in place

The ADKAR Model captures how a single person goes through change. Awareness includes the nature of the change and why the change is happening. Desire is that personal choice to embrace the change and commit to moving forward. Knowledge includes education and training on how to change (behaviors, skills, processes) and implement the change effectively. Ability is the demonstrated proficiency with new tools, processes and job roles such that the desired outcomes of the change are achieved. Reinforcement includes reward, recognition, compensation or other performance management activities that sustain the change for that person.

You can diagram this individual change process as shown in Figure 6.

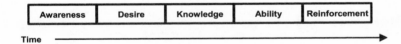

Figure 6 - ADKAR® change elements

When using this model, consider that some individuals change faster or slower than others. In other words, the time it takes for each individual to go through each phase is different, and the time it takes for the entire process is also different (see Figure 7). Change management models, therefore, cannot treat the organization as a homogeneous mass of people all going through the change process at the same rate.

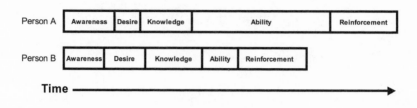

Figure 7 - Individual change progress

Now consider that each person does not find out about the change at the same time. This is especially true for large-scale changes with geographically dispersed organizations. The resulting diagram (shown in Figure 8 for a small group of employees) illustrates the actual profile of individual change for that group.

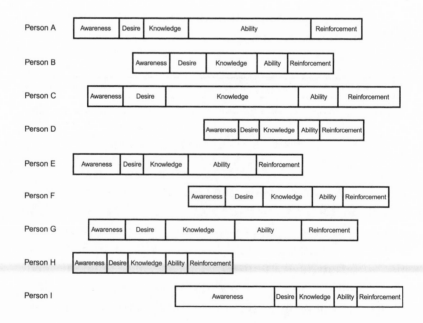

Figure 8 - Organizational ADKAR® profile

Given this organization's ADKAR profile, you can imagine how change management processes or activities that treat the organization as a uniform group are not as effective as they could be. Individuals are going through the change at their own pace. Generic, organization-wide change management activities can miss the mark entirely by focusing energy and effort in the wrong areas at the wrong time. This is especially true for communications and training for large change projects. The result of ignoring the individual component of change is that some groups are left behind, and in many cases, the timing and content of messages is poor. Individual change management must be part of the overall program.

Speed of the change process

A final observation for the concept that *change is a process* is to match the speed that employees navigate the change process to the speed of the business change. Figure 9 illustrates these two processes.

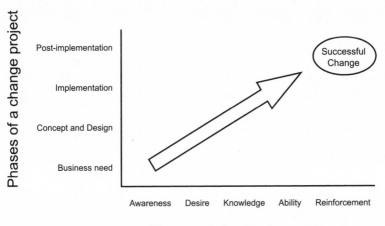

Phases of change for employees

Figure 9 - Alignment of ADKAR® with business change

On the vertical axis of the figure, the standard phases of a business change are listed. On the horizontal axis, the standard phases of personal change are shown. Successful change is defined at the upper right hand corner of this model. At this point, the business change has been fully implemented, and employees have the awareness, desire, knowledge and ability to implement those changes.

Effective changes progress along these two axes at the same time. We must manage the implementation of the technical solution and the people side of the change concurrently. If we fail to manage these two components together, then we can experience the failure points shown in Figure 10. Failure A occurs when more attention is paid to the business change and little or no attention is paid to the employees who are affected by the change. The result is higher turnover, loss of valued employees, reduced productivity and delays in the project. In many cases the change fails to produce business results. For example, Failure A could occur if a new software package was introduced with a 1-hour training class the same day the software was to be used. If this training event was all the change management that was conducted, employees will not likely pay attention to the training because they lacked awareness of why the change was happening. The new software package, even though better than its predecessor in design, will be less successful because the change process for employees was ignored.

Failure B occurs when the focus on employees is so extreme that the business change is not implemented fully and business results are not achieved. This failure mode is possible when the resistance from employees is sufficiently great as to cause the project team to dilute the change to make it more acceptable to employees. An example is when a design team becomes so concerned

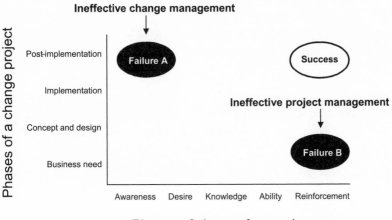

Phases of change for employees

Figure 10 - Potential failure points

about the needs and desires of employees, they lose sight of the business needs and what is right for the company, and they end up changing the solution only to reduce resistance to the change. The net effect of this action is compromised results. Either failure point is unacceptable from a business perspective. Success is achieved when a business change is introduced, employees have the awareness and desire to implement the change, the knowledge and ability to make it happen, and the reinforcement to keep the change in place.

The concept of change as a process generates multiple lessons for change management teams. Managers and senior leaders must avoid treating changes as a single meeting or announcement. Change management activities must be tailored according to where you are in the change, and be ongoing through the transition phase.

Summary of change concepts

This chapter highlighted key change concepts and how they relate to managing change in the workplace. These theories and principles are essential for managing change with situational awareness and then making the necessary adjustments, including scaling or modifying the change management process. Understanding and applying these concepts will help you correctly apply the techniques and processes for individual and organizational change management. In summary, the key concepts are:

1. Change agents must be conscious of both a sender's meaning and a receiver's interpretation.

2. Employee resistance is the norm, not the exception. Expect some employees to never support the change.

3. Visible and active sponsorship is not only desirable, but necessary for success.

4. Value systems and the culture of the organization have a direct impact on how employees react to change.

5. The size and type of the change determines how much and what kind of change management is needed. Just because a change is small does not mean that change management is unnecessary.

6. The "right" answer is not enough to implement change successfully and does little to mitigate resistance.

7. Employees go through the change process in stages and go through these stages as individuals.

To put these concepts into practice, two change management approaches are necessary: The employee's perspective and the managers perspective. Managing change with a specific employee is called individual change management. Managing change with an entire group or collection of employees is called organizational change management.

Individual change management is often overlooked by many change management models. Individual change management includes the tools and processes that supervisors use with their employees to manage individual transitions through change. This employee-oriented component of change management is the critical ingredient that allows a project team to:

1. Help employees through the change process

2. Create a feedback loop to business leaders and identify points of resistance

3. Diagnose gaps in communications and training

4. Implement corrective action

Change ultimately happens one person at a time. Each person either chooses to engage in the change, or to resist. Each person either decides to embrace the change quickly, or wait and see what happens. Each person either develops the new skills and abilities, or they struggle to work in the new environment. The collective result of these individual transitions is what produces the desired outcomes or results from the change.

The most powerful change management strategies combine organizational change management techniques with individual change management tools to create a robust, closed-loop process to manage the people side of change. Chapter 3 introduces the process and tools for individual change management. Chapter 4 integrates these tools with organizational change management techniques resulting in an overall process for managing change.

References

1. Prosci. (2012). *Best Practices in Change Management*. Loveland, Colorado: Prosci Learning Center Publications.

2. Prosci. (2012). *Best Practices in Change Management*. Loveland, Colorado: Prosci Learning Center Publications.

3. Conner, D. (1993). *Managing at the Speed of Change*. New York City, New York: Random House.

4. Prosci. (2012). *Best Practices in Change Management*. Loveland, Colorado: Prosci Learning Center Publications.

5. Block, P. (1993). *Stewardship*. San Francisco, California: Berrett-Koehler Publishers.

6. Prosci. (2012). *Best Practices in Change Management*. Loveland, Colorado: Prosci Learning Center Publications.

7. Bridges, W. (1980). *Transitions* (2nd ed.). New York City, New York: Perseus Publishing.

8. Beckhard, R., & Harris, R. (1977). *Organizational Transitions*. Reading, Massachusettes: Addison-Wesley.

CHAPTER 3

Individual change management

Individual change management is the application of tools and processes to enable employees to manage their personal transitions through change. This includes training for managers and supervisors to equip them with the tools they need to assist their employees through the change process.

This chapter shows how the ADKAR® Model[1] can be used as an individual change management tool. You will have the opportunity to create an ADKAR profile for someone close to you as a rapid way to learn the model using a personal example.

The chapter will be dedicated to four change management objectives that can be achieved using this individual change management approach:

- **Manage personal transitions**. Individuals can assess where they are in the change process and identify their own personal barriers to change.

- **Focus conversations**. Communications with employees can be targeted to where they are in the change process, thereby enabling productive and focused conversations centered on their area of interest or conflict.

- **Diagnose gaps**. Collective input from employees provides a diagnosis of why a change may be failing or is not as effective as planned.

- **Identify corrective actions**. A framework can be created to identify corrective actions during the change process.

Using ADKAR for individual change management

The ADKAR Model presents five stages that individuals go through when making a change:

- **Awareness** of the need to change

- **Desire** to participate in and support the change

- **Knowledge** about how to change

- **Ability** to implement new skills and behaviors

- **Reinforcement** to keep the change in place

This model identifies both the stages and sequence required for an individual to experience successful change. In the following pages we provide an exercise and a case study to illustrate this model. In teaching this approach, we have found that this exercise is the fastest way to become familiar with the ADKAR Model.

Exercise

Consider a change in behavior you would like to see with a friend, family member or work associate. Select a change in behavior that, up to now, you have been unable to make happen. Using the worksheets in Appendix B, rate each area on a scale of 1 to 5. A score of "1" means that you are giving this area the lowest score (e.g., a score of 1 for awareness means that you believe the person is completely unaware of the reasons a change is needed). A score of "5" indicates the highest degree of compliance or understanding for that area. Be sure you select a behavior change, which you have been trying to support in a friend, colleague or family member, that *is not working*. The worksheets in Appendix B include the following activities.

Briefly describe the personal change in behavior you are trying to facilitate with a friend, family member or work associate:

1. **Awareness.** List the reasons you believe the change is necessary. Review these reasons and rate the degree to which this person is aware of the reasons or need to change (see rating scale in Appendix B).

2. **Desire.** List the factors or consequences (good and bad) for this person that create a desire to change. Consider these motivating factors, including the person's conviction in these factors and the

associated consequences. Rate this person's desire to change.

3. **Knowledge**. List the skills and knowledge needed to support the change, including if the person has a clear picture of what the change looks like. Rate this person's knowledge or level of training in these areas.

4. **Ability**. Considering the skills and knowledge needed to change, evaluate the person's ability to perform these skills or act on this knowledge. Rate this person's ability to implement the new skills, knowledge and behaviors to support the change. Are there any barriers preventing this person from acting?

5. **Reinforcement**. List the reinforcements that will help to retain the change. Are incentives in place to reinforce the change and make it stick? Rate how well the reinforcements help support the change.

See Appendix B for complete worksheets.

Once you have completed the worksheets, consider the first area in which the score was a "3" or below. This area is referred to as the barrier point and is the first area where action must be taken.

Many people prefer to see their results in a graphical format. You can create an ADKAR profile for your results by simply making a bar graph as shown in Figure 11. In this example, the barrier point is *desire* in the first profile and *ability* in the second profile.

If you identified *awareness* as the area with a "3" or lower score for your change, then working on desire, knowledge or skill development will not facilitate the change. The first step is to communicate the reasons the change is necessary. Recall the sender and receiver model from Chapter 2 when working on this step.

On the other hand, if you identified *desire* as the first stage of the model with a score of "3" or below, then continually repeating your reasons for change will not produce forward progress and may only cause aggravation. Once a person has awareness of the need for change, you must address their inherent desire to change. Desire to change is influenced by many factors including a person's perception of the negative consequences or risk of

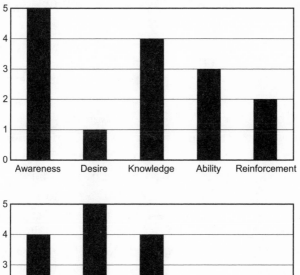

Figure 11 - Sample profiles from ADKAR® worksheet

not changing, the positive benefits, the likelihood they would be successful with the change, and other personal factors related to age, health, financial position, relationships and career status.

If *knowledge* was the area you identified, then you want to be careful not to dwell on the motivating factors. This could be discouraging for someone already at this phase. What is needed is education and training for the skills and behaviors that are required by the change.

If *ability* was the area selected with the low score, then two elements are required to move forward.

- The person will need time to develop the new skills and behaviors. Just like learning a new sport or any new skill, time is required to develop new abilities.

- The person will need ongoing coaching and support. No one-time training event or educational program will substitute for ongoing coaching and mentoring.

In certain cases, external intervention may be required to remove barriers that prevent a person from implementing the change. These barriers could be physical or psychological obstacles that require external assistance.

Finally, if *reinforcement* was the area identified, then you will need to investigate if the necessary elements are present to keep the person from reverting back to old behaviors. You would need to address the incentives or consequences for not acting in the new way.

For example, a good friend in our neighborhood has a yard full of junk. To protect his identity, we will call him "Scott." Almost every neighborhood has one of these individuals who loves to collect anything and everything, and leave it lying around. At every party, he was affectionately called "Sanford" (from the old TV show "Sanford and Son," starring Redd Foxx, in which Fred Sanford ran a junk yard).

He was definitely aware that his neighbors noticed the junk, as they often asked him when that "stuff" would disappear. In the *awareness* category, he received a score of 5. On the *desire* front, Scott was hesitant to take any action. He had no compelling reasons to relocate this treasure chest of items. Going to garage sales was entertainment for Scott. He would definitely score a 1 on desire. In terms of *knowledge* and *ability*, Scott was on a first-name basis with many auction companies and individuals who would happily come by and take the collection off his hands. Locating trash removal companies to remove the remaining garbage would be easy for Scott. In both knowledge and ability, Scott would score a 5. In terms of *reinforcement*, Scott's score diminished rapidly. Whenever a neighbor was missing a "this" or a "that," they would go to Scott for help since he collected many of the common things that we all need. And then they would thank him for having the part they were looking for. Reinforcement scores a 1, thanks to the same neighbors who wanted the mess to be cleaned up. Overall Scott's scores were 5,1,5,5,1 (see Figure 12).

Since desire was the first area below a 3, that would be the area to work first. But since this was Scott's pastime, creating desire was a large challenge. It so happened that Scott had a daughter approaching high school graduation, and Scott was looking forward to the graduation party. He had great plans to have everyone over to celebrate this wonderful event and talked repeatedly with her about how much he looked forward to this party. As graduation approached, Scott's daughter had still not invited anyone to the party. Scott became wor-

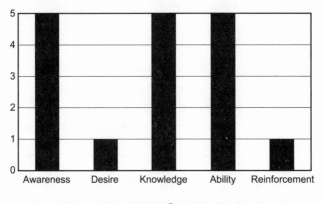

Figure 12 - ADKAR® profile for Scott

ried. Time was running out. If she did not start sending invitations, it would be too late. Finally Scott sat down with her and asked if she was ever going to mail the invitations. With tears in her eyes, she finally told him that she would be embarrassed to have anyone over to their house for graduation because of the junk everywhere.

In a heartbeat, Scott's score for desire went from a 1 to a 5. After one week and multiple trips to the junk yard, Scott had completely cleared his yard of the years of collectibles. The party went on as planned.

For Scott, his personal obstacle to change was desire. For every person, the change barrier will be unique depending on their situation and the change itself. The purpose of the personal exercise you completed earlier in this chapter and Scott's story is to introduce the ADKAR Model as a framework for looking at individual change management and how you can manage individual transitions. With this framework you can help an individual transition through change. You can also use this model as a communication framework, as a diagnostic tool and as a way to identify corrective action for business changes.

ADKAR as a communication framework

Too often business leaders fall into the trap of communicating broad and general messages about change. Employees' reactions are mixed and varied, as they each interpret those communications differently. The resulting conversations are non-targeted and often unproductive. Take, for example, the announcement of a new software tool for customer order taking. If the change is implemented and employees believe it was not needed (i.e., they were not aware that any changes were required), then their reaction might be:

"This is a waste of time."

"Why change if it was working just fine before?"

"They never tell us what's going on!"

"Our old system was better than this one."

The natural reaction to change, even in the best circumstances, is to resist. Awareness of the business need to change is a critical ingredient of any change and must come first.

If someone had taken the time to create the initial awareness of why the change was needed, the resulting dialogue would change. In this example, if the management team had explained that the old software would no longer be supported by the vendor and that new software was necessary to meet the needs of customers, then employee reaction, based on this awareness, would likely be very different:

"How soon will this happen?"

"How will this impact me?"

"Will I receive new training?"

The ADKAR Model provides focus for conversations about change. It gets at the heart of the matter quickly. Using the framework of the ADKAR Model, you can clarify communications to center on the most relevant topic and avoid unproductive conversations. Having a framework for change helps a business leader avoid sending the wrong messages or spending time on the wrong topics.

The stages of the model can also be used to identify when objections to the change are actually not objections to the design or the solution, but simply resistance to change. When engaging in a debate with an employee about the change, it is often difficult to distinguish legitimate concerns over the new solution from simple resistance to new ways of doing things. When this is occurring, you can step back from the debate about the solution and ask specific questions:

Around awareness:
"Do you understand and agree with the business reasons for making this change?"

Around desire:
"Do you want this change to happen or would you prefer to keep things the way they are? What would cause you to want this change to happen?"

Around knowledge:
"Do you know how to change and the required

skills to support the change?"

Around ability:
"Are you capable of performing these new skills?"

Around reinforcement:
*"Are you receiving the necessary support and
reinforcement to sustain this change?"*

These types of questions can isolate a potential gap or
trouble spot and change the conversation from a general
complaint about the change to a targeted conversation.
Approaching change without an individual change management model is like trying to describe a photograph
without using shapes or colors. Without a common framework and reference point, conversations can quickly
become unproductive.

ADKAR as a diagnostic tool

To be effective as a change leader, you need to determine
if your change management efforts are succeeding and
diagnose problem areas. If individual change management is being used concurrently with organizational
change management techniques, then you can create an
effective process for gathering diagnostic feedback.

Consider the ADKAR profile data that was presented
for Scott earlier in this chapter or that you generated
from your personal ADKAR exercise. Now imagine having
that type of data for 10, 100 or 1000 employees. If supervisors and managers are using individual change management tools like ADKAR with their employees, then a
systematic analysis of this data is invaluable to the

change management effort. From a diagnostic perspective, the change management team can identify trends and patterns from this data. It is not even necessary to have names of individual employees. Supervisors and managers can assist by simply providing general data for their groups.

Armed with this information, the change management team can diagnose the biggest gaps in its change management efforts. In some cases, these gaps may be localized to certain groups or departments. In other cases, these gaps may have resulted from misinformation or unclear messages from managers. For example, if you were working with multiple departments on a major change initiative, by collecting data from the ADKAR assessments you may discover that Department A is dealing with issues around awareness and desire, while Departments B and C are dealing with knowledge and ability issues of their employees. The net effect of this data analysis is a structured feedback or measurement process that allows you to understand and identify gaps in the change management process.

ADKAR as a corrective action tool

After collecting feedback on change management activities, finding the root cause for employee resistance is the first step to identifying corrective action. The stages of the ADKAR Model provide a high-level framework for categorizing feedback from employees and understanding the source of resistance. We recommend this framework because it is oriented toward the employee, and therefore the resulting corrective action is targeted at the transition stages for employees. This is a much different approach than categorizing feedback based on an organizational change management framework. In an organizational change management framework, you would likely select categories for organizing feedback like:

- Communications

- Training

- Sponsor activities

- Rewards

Unfortunately, this is structuring feedback around activities and not results. For example, saying that you need better or more communications does not accurately describe what types of communications are needed. If you use an individual change management model, the categories for organizing feedback would be:

- Awareness

- Desire

- Knowledge

- Ability

- Reinforcement

This results-oriented framework will provide the necessary direction for creating corrective action plans and activities. For example, if you determine that a major gap is knowledge about the change itself and the required new skills, then you can develop the appropriate communication and training plans to correct this knowledge gap. Project teams that can maintain a results orientation are in a better position to develop and implement corrective action based on the root cause of employee resistance.

Individual change management summary

This chapter introduced the ADKAR Model of individual change management and how it can be used in an organization. Individual change management is valuable to:

- Manage personal transitions and use as a coaching tool for managers to use with their employees

- Focus conversations, especially when dealing with resistant employees

- Diagnose gaps in the change management program for each group or department

- Identify corrective actions based on specific desired results

The process for using individual change management tools like ADKAR begins with training for managers and supervisors. These front-line coaches are a critical component of individual change management. In many cases, these managers and supervisors will be the "trainers" for their groups when it is not feasible for your company to train every employee about change management.
    The central activities of individual change manage-

ment are assessments and individual coaching. Both the employees and the supervisors need to be aware of their role and how to participate in individual change management. Worksheets for a business change, like those provided in Appendix B, are key components of this assessment and coaching process.

The final activities in individual change management include data collection, root-cause analysis and corrective action based on this data. Through this process the change management team can determine what is working and what is not, and take the necessary steps. This feedback process is the integration point between individual change management and organizational change management, as presented in Chapter 4.

Getting started

The first step to applying individual change management with employees is to provide supervisors and managers with training and tools. This training will provide a solid understanding of the activities and worksheets that should be used in team meetings and individual coaching sessions.

ADKAR training, worksheets and guidelines for applying individual change management with employees are available at the Change Management Learning Center at www.change-management.com. Specifically for managers, a resource called the "*Change Management Guide for Managers*" is available that details how the ADKAR Model is used with their teams. See Appendix A for more details.

References

1. Hiatt, J. (2006). *ADKAR: A model for change in business, government and our community*. Loveland, Colorado: Prosci Learning Center Publications.

CHAPTER 4

Organizational change management

Businesses tend to have more managers who believe they have the right answers to business problems than managers who can effectively implement good ideas. As a leadership competency, change management is often lacking. The political environment, combined with employee resistance, stops many managers from being true leaders of change.

In this chapter we provide an overview of a comprehensive, research-based change management process that can be a starting point for developing this competency. We will discuss how individual change management tools and organization-wide techniques can be combined to effectively manage change.

Based on Prosci's research in change management over the course of seven separate studies with more than 2600 organizations, the most effective change management process consists of three phases including:

Phase 1 - Preparing for change

Phase 2 - Managing change

Phase 3 - Reinforcing change™

This chapter provides an introduction to this process as shown in Figure 13 and summarizes the key steps. Phase 1 focuses on understanding the change and the organization impacted by the change, and then developing a change management strategy. Phase 2 is the time for planning and action. Phase 3 is the time for reinforcing the change and celebrating success.

Phase 1 - Preparing for change includes activities to prepare yourself and your team for managing the change, to prepare business leaders to support the change and to create a high-level change management strategy. This first phase of change management activities can be considered a "getting-ready" period. During this phase, you will:

- Assess the scope of the change, including: *How big is this change? How many people are affected? Is it a gradual or radical change?*

- Assess the readiness of the organization impacted by the change, including: *What are the value systems and backgrounds of the impacted groups? How much change is already going on? What type of resistance can be expected? What is their history with change?*

- Acquire project resources and assess the strengths of your change management team.

- Assess the sponsor coalition and take the first steps to enable them to effectively lead the change process.

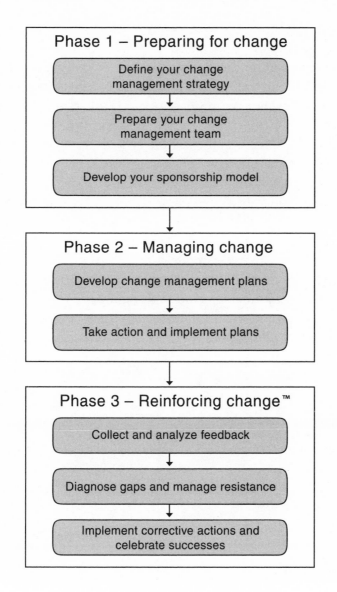

Figure 13 - Prosci® 3-Phase Change Management Process

Your change management strategy is a direct result of these assessments and the degree of risk you face. For example, a large, radical change made to a large, "change-resistant" organization will entail more project risk and require more change management. Conversely, a small change made to a single department or group will require less change management and fewer activities (see Figure 14). The initial assessment tells you the depth and breadth of the change management effort.

Given this initial assessment, you can make fundamental strategy decisions related to the project. These decisions will impact your change management team structure and sponsor model. In addition, the assessments of the size of the change and the organizational attributes will guide decision making during the planning process for communications, training, coaching and sponsor activities. This scaling and customization effort is what makes change management effective.

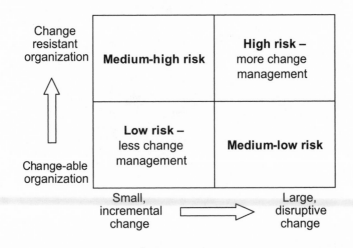

Figure 14 - Change management scaling

Once the change management strategy is set, you can select and prepare a change management team. These team members are selected and trained prior to creating detailed change management plans. Depending on the outcome of the initial assessments, the change management team may be as small as one part-time person (yourself) or as large as a core team with several sub-teams.

Concurrent with preparing the change management team, a sponsor model is selected. A sponsor model is the desired support structure of business leaders necessary to charter, authorize and lead the change. Sponsor models can be as large as a steering committee of key executives or as small as one project champion working with the project team. This decision is based on the size of the change and the nature of the organization that is changing.

Along with the selection of a sponsor model, your business leaders and stakeholders (any individual or group who has processes, systems or people affected by the change) are evaluated based on their support or opposition to the change. This assessment provides you with a benchmark of "who's who?" and "where do they stand?" This is the starting point for building sponsorship for the change throughout the organization.

Think of this preparation phase like getting ready for a trip. When making plans for a major worldwide excursion you may ask questions like: "Where are we going to travel?", "How hard is it to get there?", "Will we need special assistance or guides?", and "What visas and documents are required?" These questions and the evaluation of the answers will help your trip go smoothly. Now consider an evening trip to a local sporting event. Not only are the answers to these questions different, even the questions will change. You will scale your trip plans accordingly. Likewise, change management requires you to scale your activities. By asking questions about the change and the impacted organization, you can choose the best change management approach and team structure to fit that situation.

In the most straightforward terms, good change leaders will look at the change, their team and their sponsors and ask the question, "Do I have the right ingredients to succeed?" If not, then you need to adjust your team, enhance your sponsorship, or scale back the change. The goal is to match the degree of sponsorship with the scope of the change.

Phase 2 - Managing change includes the design of the organizational change management plans and individual change management activities. This second phase of change management involves the planning and implementation of:

- Communication plans
- Coaching plans
- Training plans
- Sponsor roadmaps
- Resistance management plans

Each of these plans and the associated activities that are often collectively referred to as Organizational Change Management are designed with one purpose in mind: to enable each employee impacted by the change to transition successfully to the desired future state so that the collective change of these individuals results in achievement of the desired outcomes or business results for the change overall.

Communication plan – Many managers assume that if they communicate clearly with their employees, their job is done. Recall from Chapter 2 and the principles of change that there are many reasons why employees may not hear or understand what their managers are saying. You may have heard that messages need to be repeated five to seven times before they are cemented into the minds of employees. That is because each employee's readiness to hear depends on the many factors discussed in Chapter 2. Effective communicators carefully consider three components: the audience, what is said and when it is said.

For example, the first step in managing change is building awareness around the need for change and creating a desire among employees (recall the Prosci® ADKAR® Model). Therefore, the initial communications should be designed to create awareness around the business reasons for change and the risk of not changing. These early communications should not be cluttered with details that will distract from the key messages. Likewise, at each step in the process, communications should be designed to share the right messages at the right time.

Communication planning, therefore, begins with a careful analysis of the audiences, key messages and the timing for those messages. The change management team must design a communication plan that addresses the needs of front-line employees, supervisors and executives. Each audience has particular needs for information based on its role in the implementation of the change. As a starting point, the following communication checklist taken from the *Prosci® Change Management Toolkit*[1] provides a summary of the most important communication topics for managing change.

Messages about the business today (shared during the earliest stages of the change)

- The current situation and the rationale for the change
- The business issues or drivers that created a need for change
- Competitive issues or changes in the marketplace including customer issues
- Financial issues or trends
- What might happen if a change is not made (the risk of not making the change)

Messages about the change (shared after employees understand the business situation and business reasons for the change)

- A vision of the organization after the change takes place
- Scope of the change (including process scope, organizational scope, systems and technology scope)
- Objectives for the change, including a definition of success
- Alignment of the change with the business strategy
- How big of a change is needed (how big is the gap between today and the future state)
- Who is most impacted and who is least impacted
- The basics of what is changing, how it will change, and when it will change, including what will not change

Messages about how the change impacts employees (shared concurrently with messages about the change)

- The expectation that change will happen and is not a choice
- The impact of the change on the day-to-day activities of each employee
- WIIFM - "What's in it for me?" - from an employee's perspective
- Implications of the change on job security
- Specific behaviors and activities expected from employees
- Procedures for getting help and assistance during the change
- Ways to provide feedback

The schedule for the project overall (shared when available)

- The overall time frame for the change
- When new information will be available
- How information about the project will be shared
- Major milestones and deliverables
- Key decision points
- Early success stories

Coaching plan – Supervisors and managers will play a key role in the change management program. Ultimately, the direct supervisor has more influence over an employee's motivation to change than any other person at work. Unfortunately, supervisors as a group can be the most difficult to convince of the need for change and can be a source of resistance themselves. It is vital for the change management team and executive sponsors to gain the support of supervisors and to build change leadership. Individual change management activities as discussed in

Chapter 3 should be used to help supervisors through the change process.

Once managers and supervisors are on board, the change management team must prepare a coaching strategy. They will need to provide training for supervisors including how to use individual change management tools with their employees. Ultimately, it is not change management professionals or HR personnel who coach employees through change. It is the direct supervisor for each employee who acts as the change manager and coach through change.

Training plan – Training is the cornerstone for building knowledge about the change and the required skills. Project team members will develop training requirements based on the skills, knowledge and behaviors necessary to implement the change. These training requirements will be the starting point for the training group or the project team to develop training programs.

Sponsor roadmap – Business leaders and executives play a critical sponsor role in change management. The change management team must develop a plan for sponsor activities and help key business leaders carry out these plans. In fact, research has consistently pointed to sponsorship as the most important success factor. Avoid confusing the notion of sponsorship with support. The CEO of the company may support your project, but that is not the same as sponsoring your initiative. Sponsorship involves active and visible participation by senior business leaders throughout the process.

Unfortunately, many executives do not know what this sponsorship looks like. Your role includes helping senior executives do the right things to sponsor the project. Details on preparing sponsor plans and communications for executives can be found in the *Prosci® Change Management Toolkit* (see Appendix A for more information).

Resistance management plan — Resistance from employees and managers is normal. Persistent resistance, however, can threaten a project. The change management team needs to identify, understand and manage resistance throughout the organization using the techniques outlined in Chapter 3 for individual change management.

Pulling it all together

Each of these plans and activities must be customized based on your change and the unique attributes of your organization. Once the change management team has completed the planning process, implementation begins. In reality, it is never as clean as Step A, Step B, Step C and so on. Most teams are implementing some plans while creating and adjusting others. If you are starting change management in the middle of a project, you could be implementing some activities before the plans are even finalized. The fact is that projects move forward with or without you. Messages are being sent every day that may help or hurt the change. Key stakeholders throughout the organization will continue to communicate with their employees whether or not the change management team is ready. Some of their messages will help manage the change forward, others may block progress.

In the trip analogy, *Phase 2 — Managing change* is equivalent to creating detailed checklists, packing up and heading out. You will need to determine the how, when and who of each aspect of your journey. The more complex the trip, the more detail and care you will take in this stage. Checklists become critical to ensure that key items like tickets and passports are not forgotten. Integrating change management into project management occurs at this phase. At some point you depart. This is when your plans turn into reality and the trip begins. In the *Managing change* phase, you will create change management plans and implement those plans for your project.

However, we all know that not every aspect of a trip goes as planned. Unexpected events including the weather, car trouble, cancelled flights or congested highways can result in the need for course corrections. In these situations we review the plans, make alternate arrangements and continue onward. For change management, this is the role of Phase 3.

In *Phase 3 – Reinforcing change*, you will assess the results of the change management activities and implement corrective action. This phase also includes celebrating early successes, conducting "after-action reviews" and transferring ownership of the change from the change management team to the organization.

This reinforcement phase begins with an assessment of the results of the change management activities by collecting feedback from employees. The data collection process also includes compliance audits to determine if the new processes and tools are being used properly. For simple changes, this process is as straightforward as listening and watching. These assessment results form the basis for corrective action plans and resistance management activities. The change management team analyzes the results of the feedback and compliance audits, determines the root cause of key problems and creates plans to correct these problems.

Celebrating successes, especially early wins for the project, is a critical component of change management. The change management team, however, must actively seek out these early successes and arrange for the recognition of these events. Too often, projects overlook the importance of celebrating achievements with employees.

The transition of the overall change process to the operational managers of the organization enables the managers running the day-to-day operation to take control. They will assume the role of reinforcing the change and rewarding ongoing performance.

The final step in the change management process is the after-action review. It is at this point that you can stand back from the entire program, evaluate successes and failures, and identify process changes for the next project. This is part of the ongoing, continuous improvement of change management for your organization and ultimately leads to change competency.

One of the biggest mistakes many change management teams make is not completing this third phase of managing change. In some cases, change management activities are stopped after initial communications and training activities are finished. This approach does not complete the process of change management and can ultimately result in the same types of failure that come from no change management at all.

Managing the people side of change, whether on a large company-wide consolidation project or with a very small change project, does not require difficult or complex steps. What is required is the application of a thoughtful process for managing the change that is customized for the size and complexity of each project. The three phases introduced in this chapter form the framework for this type of structured change management process. We have presented a very brief outline of these steps in this chapter, but you will need more than an overview to implement these plans effectively. See Appendix A for more information.

Avoiding damage control and "fire fighting"

Following a structured process for managing change is most effective when it begins at the same time that the business change begins. However, the reality in today's environment is that change management is not always initiated at the start of a new project. In many cases managers rush to implement change management tactics only after problems surface. The result is frantic work to control the damage and to put out "fires."

Since not all projects begin using change management at the onset, you may need to adjust your approach depending on where you are in the project lifecycle. As a change management leader or consultant, you may find yourself in several entry-point scenarios.

1. The project has just started and change management will be applied from the very beginning. This typically occurs when you, someone from your team or your project sponsor brings change management to the project as a required discipline. This is the best-case scenario.

2. The project team has completed the planning and solution design activities and has decided to apply change management now that implementation is starting. Existing team structures and roles are defined and change management is being layered onto an existing process.

3. The project is well underway and implementation has already begun. The project team is already experiencing resistance to the change. Change management is a reaction to the issues created by this resistance. This is the worst-case scenario.

The importance of entry points for change management is twofold. First, the later in the project you begin change management activities, the more difficult the task of managing change becomes. It is easier to prevent than fix. When starting late, your initial work will most likely be damage control. Second, many change management models are prescriptive (i.e., recipe driven). This can be a problem if your step-by-step process assumes that you are starting at the beginning, when really you are jumping in at the middle of a project. Your understanding of change management principles will be critical for success in this situation.

If you are asked to implement change management in a project that is already underway, be aware that you will need to spend considerable time evaluating what has already been communicated to employees, both directly and indirectly. You will also have to review the existing sponsor model and training programs to determine gaps and to identify any misinformation that may have been shared about the change. An individual change management approach like ADKAR is useful for assessing and correcting these types of situations.

As an organization gains competency in managing change, the practices and techniques of change management are initiated earlier. If you are in a position to influence your business projects, the most significant recommendation you can make is to have change management be a required practice at the beginning of every new project. When change management becomes part of "business as usual" the organization begins to build change competency as described in Chapter 5.

Connecting change management and business improvement methodologies

Many processes exist for improving business performance. A common problem of project managers is figuring out how to connect their business improvement program with change management. Examples of business improvement programs include:

- Merger or acquisition

- Six Sigma

- Business Process Reengineering (BPR)

- Total Quality Management (continuous improvement)

- Restructuring or reorganization

- Organization Development interventions (OD)

In addition, consulting firms bring their own methods and processes for diagnosing and solving business problems. All of these business improvement approaches can and should use change management.

First and foremost, change management and project management should be approached hand in hand, with change management activities fully integrated into the project plan. Second, these business improvement programs should be viewed as mechanisms to identify and define the change itself, not as a method of managing that change with employees. Finally, the application of change management does not need to wait until the solution is fully defined. In fact, the sooner change management can begin, the greater the probability for success.

For example, consider a generic business improvement process that includes:

Business improvement process steps

1. Problem or opportunity identification

2. Project planning and team formation

3. Data gathering and business solution design

4. Process design, system development and organization design

5. Implementation and measurement

Likewise, most change management models include some of the following elements as discussed here in Chapter 4.

Change management components

A. Organization and change assessments

B. Team readiness and sponsor preparation

C. Awareness building, communications and training

D. Coaching, feedback and employee involvement

E. Resistance management

In the best-case scenario, when the starting point for change management is at the start of the project, you can embed the change management steps and activities discussed in this chapter with the business improvement steps (see Figure 15). In this model, the overall process becomes a seamless integration of both the improvement process and the change management process. The opportunity, for example, of employee involvement in the change process is greatly enhanced if you begin change management early in the process. Employee participation becomes a core strategy for gaining employee support and buy-in, and results in a better overall solution.

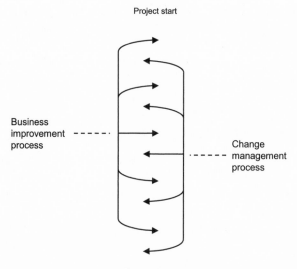

Figure 15 - Integration of change management

Conversely, if change management begins later, the process is typically an overlay of change management practices on top of existing project activities. In this situation, the ability to integrate activities presents a greater challenge (see Figure 16). Resistance may already be present. Change management serves as a tool to fix the current problems and avoid similar issues in the future. Integration with the business improvement activities and team structure is difficult this late in the process.

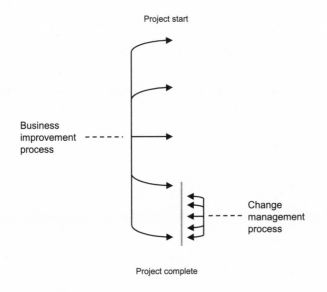

Figure 16 - Change management layering

Each scenario presents different challenges to the change management team and requires the change management process to be flexible to meet the needs of the business.

Organizational change management summary

Organizational change management is a management responsibility. It involves using communications, training, coaching, sponsorship and resistance management to enable individual change. Tools like ADKAR help guide the planning and assessment of organizational change management activities so that the final outcome is achievement of business results. In many cases when you have been chartered with change management, the expectation may only be a few communications or perhaps a training program. This is a false expectation and may require re-calibrating your organization and business leaders to what change management is and why it is important. Robust change management includes communication and training, but also includes the tools and processes for building effective sponsorship, enabling supervisors to lead change with their employees and managing resistance. Finally, good change management processes close the loop by including listening to employees, developing corrective action programs and celebrating successes.

Reconnecting with business results

One of the most important conclusions you should draw from these first four chapters about change management is that we manage the people side of change for one primary reason: to achieve business results. A useful exercise to cement that thinking is to follow the following thought process:

1. Why are we making this change? What are the specific outcomes or results we are trying to achieve?

2. What specifically needs to change to enable us to meet our objectives? When answering this question, consider processes, systems and tools, facilities, organizational models, and job roles.

3. Who needs to change? What groups, departments, divisions are impacted by this change?

When you have the answers to these questions, you can then work the thought process backwards. If I am unsuccessful in realizing change with those employees in the organization impacted by the change, I will not successfully implement the new processes, systems or job roles. If I am unable to implement these critical components of the change, then I will not achieve the desired outcomes of the change.

In other words, business results and managing the people side of change are inseparable. That is why change management is more than simply communications or training. Change management is a leadership competency that enables organizations to respond to changing market conditions so they can adapt, grow and be profitable. Change management enables business results to be realized from the change initiatives you have designed for your organization. It is the connection between business outcomes and change management that resonates the loudest with business leaders and executives.

References

1. Prosci. (2012). *Prosci Change Management Toolkit.* Loveland, Colorado: Prosci Learning Center Publications.

CHAPTER 5

Change competency

Throughout this book, the term change management has been used in relation to managing change with one or more business initiatives. But what happens when change becomes the norm? Current economic conditions have placed a premium on an organization's ability to be flexible, quick-to-market, scalable and responsive to unique customer demands.

An organization that faces constant demands to change and uses effective change management over and over with each new initiative may experience a fundamental shift in its operations and the behavior of its employees. Sponsors begin to repeat activities that made the last change successful. Managers develop skills to support employees through the change. Employees see part of their job as navigating these new changes. Each level in the organization will have internalized its role in change and developed the skills and knowledge necessary to react to constant change. The organization has become ready and able to embrace change; it has developed change competency.

Building change competency in an organization is not like installing a new computer system or implementing a new procedure. Change competency requires a new attitude and approach. Individuals in a change-competent organization define their job in relation to change. They value the ability to change as one of their primary responsibilities. They understand that change will occur, expect it and support the change during implementation.

Change competency is the infusion of a business culture that expects change and reacts with the understanding, perspectives, tools and techniques to make change seamless and effortless. It is making change a part of "business as usual."

Change competency is similar to change management, but there are several key distinctions. First, change management is the application of tools and processes to manage the people side of change on a specific project so that the desired outcomes of that change are realized. Change competency is not project specific; it is an organization's capability to manage the people side of change on all change initiatives, and includes the competencies of executives, managers and employees throughout the organization.

Second, while change management can be taught and learned, change competency requires a fundamental shift in culture and values. It must become part of day-to-day operations and cannot be simply demonstrated in training or instructional material.

Third, change competency must penetrate every facet and level of the organization. This distinction especially relates to the front-line employees. An organization may have expertise in change management in its sponsors, consultants and change management practitioners. However, the front-line employees are the ones whose day-to-day activities are changing. In change management, these employees are the target of much of the activity. In change-competent organizations, these employees are key participants. They must be given the perspectives, tools and techniques to rapidly and successfully change for the organization to build change competency.

Although a main focus of organizational change management, employees are often neglected when it comes to building competency in change. Training and resources are readily available for executives, change teams, and even managers and supervisors. Front-line employees, however, are often left behind. Ironically, managing employee resistance is often the number one challenge for change management teams. The importance of front-line employees should not be underestimated.

Consider an employee's role in change compared to members of a project team or the executive sponsors. For the project team, the current change initiative may be the only project they work on before they move on to other opportunities in the business. The executive sponsor of the project probably has many other decisions and initiatives to support, and this project is only a small part of the big picture. However, for the employees who must change their daily activities, this change initiative could produce dramatic and radical change to their careers. It may do away with everything they know and are comfortable with. It may introduce systems, processes or approaches that are new and intimidating. To truly build change competency into an organization, the front-line employees must understand how they can succeed and perform in a constantly changing business world.

Evidence of a change-competent organization

Change-competent organizations, as viewed from each role in the organization, have the following objectives:

Executive – constantly search for ways to improve profitability and growth by reacting to marketplace changes and opportunities, and ensuring that business changes are implemented and realized to their full potential through effective leadership and change sponsorship.

Project team – support sponsors, managers and front-line employees through the change process with tools, processes and techniques to manage change.

Managers – support employees through the change process; provide direction and steering for professional development and encourage successful performance in the new environment, including coaching employees on change management techniques.

Front-line employees – perform successfully in the current environment, during the transition and in the changed environment.

To build change competency, you must equip all levels of your organization with the understanding, perspectives and tools to make change seamless and effortless.

You can use the ADKAR Model to assess where your organization is today relative to change competency and to develop an action plan to move in that direction. Consider and evaluate the following statements as they relate to your organization. Use the assessment process presented previously in Chapter 3 for applying the

ADKAR Model. If a statement accurately reflects your current state, then you would score a 5. If a statement is in strong contrast to the current state of the organization, then you would score a 1 in that area.

Awareness – the organization understands the importance of responding quickly and efficiently to internal and external pressures to change; the organization understands what change management is and the associated business risks of not developing competencies to manage change; all groups understand the business reasons and drivers for making this shift in culture, values and skills.

Desire – all groups at all levels acknowledge that the ability to change is critical if the organization is to survive, and they are ready and willing to begin the journey toward change management competency.

Knowledge – the organization has the base knowledge of what a change capable organization looks like and what skills and values are required; all facets of the organization have a basic understanding of change management theories and practices; each group understands its role in a change-competent organization.

Ability – the organization possesses and effectively utilizes the tools and processes to manage change; leaders, change practitioners and front-line employees have practice and coaching in being successful change agents and can routinely apply their knowledge and skills to realize change; barriers that prevent change implementation are readily identified and removed.

Reinforcement – the organization encourages and

rewards successful change through its culture, values and initiatives; support of change competency is reinforced and resistance to change is identified and managed; change is part of "business as usual."

Change is a process, and building change competency will take time. It is important to realize that you will need to apply change management techniques to this change as well. You will need to recognize where you are today, where you want to be in the future, and what it will take to make that transition. You will need to consider the transition to a change-capable organization as a "change" in and of itself, and that means that you will need active and visible sponsorship, project management and change management in order to succeed.

Summary

To build change competency into your organization, you can take the first step by ensuring that solid change management practices are applied consistently for each change initiative or project. The second step is to begin building knowledge and skills in the following areas of organizational change management:

- Change management planning and strategies

- Change management team structures

- Change management roles

- Organizational change management methodologies

- Executive sponsorship strategies

- Communication planning and delivery

- Training and educational programs

- Incentive and recognition programs

For individual change competency, you will need to build knowledge and skills in the following areas:

- Methods for managing employee resistance

- Models for individual change management like ADKAR

- Coaching tools and techniques for helping employees navigate the change process

- Activities and exercises for supervisors to use with their employees to manage change

- Incentive and recognition programs

CHAPTER 6

Conclusion

Change Management: The People Side of Change presents the foundation needed to effectively manage change. Some of you may have noticed that the book itself was organized along the Prosci® ADKAR® Model for change.

The book began by creating **Awareness** of the need for change management and **Desire** to use change management techniques to avoid project failures or business disruptions. Change management is used for one reason – to ensure business success. Many changes fail in organizations because they do not appreciate and manage the people side of change. We presented research results that showed change management as the most critical and important activity for business improvement projects. There are many forms of employee and management resistance that can severely impair or stop a change project. Project teams that introduce change but do not use change management run the risk of missed project objectives, productivity losses, and sometimes complete failure.

Next, the concepts and theories of change management built the necessary **Knowledge** to be an effective change agent and to scale your change management efforts. Change management does not work with a "one-size-fits-all" approach. The best and most effective change management approach will match the specific change and the particular organization that is being changed. As a practitioner, the seven concepts of change are critical for understanding both why and how to use change management. The seven key concepts are:

1. Change leaders must be conscious of both a sender's message and a receiver's interpretation.

2. Employee resistance is the norm, not the exception.

3. Visible and active sponsorship is not only desirable but necessary for success.

4. Value systems and the culture of the organization have a direct impact on how employees react to change.

5. The size of the change determines how much and what kind of change management is needed.

6. The "right" answer is not enough to successfully implement change.

7. Employees go through the change process in stages and go through these stages as individuals.

The chapters on individual change management and organizational change management added knowledge on how to manage change. In these chapters, tools and processes were introduced to increase your **Ability** to manage change. Individual change management is the process of helping individuals understand, cope with and thrive in a changing environment. As individuals, we experience change differently. We go through change in stages. We may take longer or shorter to move through each stage, and we may start at different times. For individual change management, the ADKAR Model was introduced. ADKAR is a useful tool for focusing conversations about change, diagnosing the root causes of resistance, determining corrective actions and managing individual transitions.

Organizational change management is the manager's view of change – the process, activities and tools used within an organization to make a change successful. Organizational change management involves "Preparing for change, Managing change and Reinforcing change™" as outlined in the Prosci® 3-Phase Change Management Process. The chapter on organizational change management presented this structured process for change management and introduced the key plans and activities that are required. It is not enough to complete an activity and move on. You must assess the impact of the activity, diagnose any gaps and develop corrective actions for organizational change management to be effective.

The missteps and project failures uncovered in research with other companies provide **Reinforcement** for managing the people side of change. When change management is reinforced in your company as a necessary leadership skill, the organization begins to build competencies at each level: executives, mid-level managers and front-line employees. A change-competent organization views change as part of "business as usual." Changes are not feared and resisted, but expected and embraced. Change competency involves a shift in values, culture and operations. It is not a quick and easy competency to develop, but it is critical given the ever-changing business environment.

What is the next step?

One of your key responsibilities as a leader of change is to be the champion of change management in your organization. You must demonstrate the importance of actively managing change and build support among your peers, leaders and direct reports. You must provide guidance to senior executives, and managers and supervisors. You must help the organization thrive during and embrace change.

In the Appendices of this book you will find additional material to help with the processes of managing change and building change competency. In Appendix A, we provide a list of change management resources to help you take the next step. In Appendix B, you will find ADKAR worksheets. In Appendix C, we have included highlights from Prosci's most recent benchmarking report on change management. In Appendix D, we have listed the most commonly asked questions from employees and general answers that can serve as a starting point for your communications.

Appendices

Appendix A – Change management resources

Change management tutorials

You can register for free white papers and tutorials at www.change-management.com. Click the registration button. There is no charge for registering.

Change Management Toolkit (CD-ROM/USB and Binder)

The *Change Management Toolkit* is a comprehensive leader's guide that contains templates and guidelines to help you effectively deploy change management and write a complete and professional change management plan. Assessment tools and implementation guidelines will help you implement an effective change management strategy. The Change Management Toolkit teaches you to:

- Manage the people side of change, not just the business aspects

- Develop a change management strategy for your project

- Create customized change management plans

- Actively manage resistance to change

Toolkit components

The toolkit contains the following components:

- Change management overview – what change management is, why it is important, what I can do to manage change effectively

- Assessments – tools for evaluating your change and your organization's readiness for change

- Templates – critical document templates for planning and executing change management – provided on CD-ROM/USB

- Theories and perspectives – a practical discussion of change principles and concepts

- Change management process – guidelines, templates and checklists for the entire change management process including planning templates for communications, training and coaching

- Customization guidelines – change management should reflect your unique change and the organization that is changing; learn how to adapt to the specifics of your project

Toolkit structure

The toolkit covers the following change management phases:

Preparing for change: Build a foundation for managing change. Examine theories and perspectives that impact how people go through change. Assess your specific change characteristics and the organizational attributes that impact change management. Develop your team structure and sponsor model.

Managing change: Develop key change management plans: communications, sponsorship, coaching, training, and resistance management. Create a project plan for implementing change management activities and learn how to use the Prosci® ADKAR® Model.

Reinforcing change: Assess the effectiveness of change management activities. Identify and overcome obstacles. Build buy-in and celebrate successes.

This toolkit is also available in a fully web-enabled application called the Change Management Pilot Professional, allowing rapid access from anywhere in the world.

Products are available at www.change-management.com or by calling Prosci at +1-970-203-9332.

Best Practices in Change Management (journal-style report)

The *Best Practices in Change Management* report presents comprehensive findings from more than two thousand companies over a fourteen-year period on their experiences and lessons learned in change management. This report makes it easy to learn change management best practices and uncovers the mistakes to avoid when creating executive sponsorship. Participants share:

- How to effectively manage change

- How to combat employee resistance

- How to build executive support for your project

- What teams would do differently on their next project

Study participants include team leaders, change management advisory team members, project team members, consultants and management sponsors. The report is a compendium of research studies that repeat every two years to present the most effective and up-to-date practices in change management.

Success factors:
Uncover the greatest contributors to the success of a change management program.

Methodology:
Learn the "must do" activities for each phase of the project: planning, design and implementation.

Role of top management:
Learn which key activities sponsors can do to contribute to the success of the project, as well as the biggest mistakes they often make.

Communications:
Determine the most effective methods of communication and find out how frequently objectives and status of the project need to be communicated.

Team structure:
Learn the top criteria for a good change management team member, and how to improve the effectiveness of your change management effort by selecting the right people.

Using consultants:
Understand the key contributions that consultants make to a project and determine how to define the consultants' roles for optimum success.

Employee's Survival Guide to Change (paperback)

"The best change management guide that a business can provide to its employees."
Sandy D., Avaya

"A much needed addition to every employee's toolbox! The first thing to reach for when faced with change. It's like hiring a 'personal coach' at a fraction of the cost."
Madeleine Ashe, Vanguard Communications
Corporation

There are few tools on the market designed to help employees impacted by change. Ironically, nearly one-fourth of major change initiatives fail because employees are fearful of and resistant to change. The *Employee's Survival Guide to Change* answers questions most employees are unwilling to ask and uncovers what it takes to survive and thrive in today's changing workplace. Employees will learn the ADKAR Model and how to become effective change agents instead of difficult change barriers.

The *Employee's Survival Guide to Change* helps you:

- Avoid the loss of valued employees and minimize business disruption caused by the change

- Answer the questions employees are afraid to ask

- Describe the phases of the change and what employees can expect

- Garner support from employees who would otherwise resist the change

- Create an attitude of "can do" rather than "not my job"

Change Management Guide For Managers (CD-ROM/USB and Binder)

The *Change Management Guide for Managers* includes detailed guidelines and exercises for managers and supervisors to assist employees through the change process. Activities and worksheets are included for working with employee groups.

Use this resource with the *Employee's Survival Guide to Change* to:

- Overcome resistance and reduce employee turnover

- Avoid productivity losses caused by process, technology or organizational changes

- Lower employee stress and increase employee satisfaction

- Effectively deploy and manage change in your organization

Managing change templates
This toolkit helps managers build a change management strategy for their team. This product includes the following tools:

- Change summary worksheet

- Manager's change competency assessments

- Change management process for managers

- ADKAR® employee assessments

- Employee roadmap

- Reinforcing change checklist

Available at www.change-management.com or by calling Prosci at +1-970-203-9332.

Additional suggested reading material

Anderson, Dean and Linda Ackerman Anderson. *Beyond Change Management: Advanced Strategies for Today's Transformational Leaders.* Jossey-Bass/Pfeiffer, 2001.

Beckhard, Richard and Reuben T. Harris. *Organizational Transitions: Managing Complex Change.* Addison-Wesley Publishing Company, 1987.

Bridges, William. *Managing Transitions: Making the Most of Change.* De Capo Press, 1991.

Charan, Ram and Geoffrey Colvin. "Why CEOs Fail." Fortune. 21 June 1999.

Conner, Daryl R. *Managing at the Speed of Change.* Villard Books, 1993.

Duck, Jeanie Daniel. *The Change Monster: The Human Forces that Fuel or Foil Corporate Transformation and Change.* Three Rivers Press, 2001.

Essex, David E. "In Search of ROI." PM Network. Oct. 2005: 50.

Hiatt, Jeffrey M. *ADKAR: A Model for Change in Business, Government and Our Community.* Prosci Learning Center Publications, 2006.

Johnson, Spencer and Kenneth H. Blanchard. *Who Moved My Cheese? An Amazing Way to Deal with Change in Your Work and in Your Life.* G.P. Putnam's Sons, 1998.

Kotter, John P. *Leading Change.* Harvard Business School Press, 1996.

Kotter, John P. and Holger Rathgeber. *Our Iceberg Is Melting: Changing and Succeeding Under Any Conditions.* St. Martin's Press, 2006.

Kubler-Ross, Elisabeth. *On Death and Dying.* Touchstone, 1969.

Lamarsh, Jeanenne. *Changing the Way We Change.* Addison-Wesley Publishing Company, 1995.

LaClair, Jennifer A. and Ravi P. Rao. "Helping Employees Embrace Change." The McKinsey Quarterly. 2002: Number 4.

McClelland, David C. *Human Motivation.* Cambridge University Press, 1987.

Appendix B – ADKAR® worksheets

ADKAR worksheet for personal change

Briefly describe a **personal** change you are trying to support with a friend, family member or work associate.

1. List the reasons you believe the change is necessary.

_____
_____
_____
_____
_____
_____
_____
_____
_____
_____
_____
_____
_____
_____
_____
_____
_____

Review these reasons and rate this person's **awareness** of these reasons for change.

Score

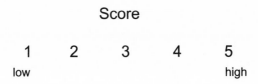

2. List the factors or consequences (good and bad) for this person that create a *desire* to change.

_____

_____

_____

_____

_____

_____

_____

_____

_____

_____

_____

_____

_____

_____

_____

_____

Consider these motivating factors, including the person's conviction in these factors and the associated consequences. Assess this person's **desire** to change.

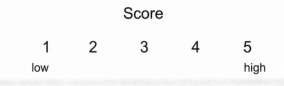

Score

1	2	3	4	5
low				high

3. List the skills and *knowledge* needed for the change.

_____

_____

_____

_____

_____

_____

_____

_____

_____

_____

_____

_____

_____

Rate this person's **knowledge** or training in these areas.

Score

1   2   3   4   5

low   high

4. Considering the skills and knowledge identified in Step 3, evaluate the person's *ability* to perform these skills or act on this knowledge.

_____

_____

_____

_____

_____

_____

_____

_____

_____

_____

_____

_____

_____

_____

To what degree do you rate this person's **ability** to implement the new skills, knowledge and behaviors to support the change?

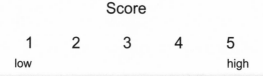

Score

1   2   3   4   5

low   high

5. List the *reinforcements* that will help to retain the change. Are incentives in place to reinforce the change and make it stick?

_____

_____

_____

_____

_____

_____

_____

_____

_____

_____

_____

_____

_____

_____

_____

_____

To what degree do you rate the **reinforcements** as helping support the change?

Score

1   2   3   4   5
low   high

Now transfer your scores from each worksheet to the table below. Take a moment to review your scores. Highlight the first area to score a 3 or lower. This is the starting point for managing change with this individual.

Brief description of the change:

1. **Awareness** of the need to change?

                                  1   2   3   4   5

Notes:_____

2. **Desire** to make the change happen?

                                  1   2   3   4   5

Notes:_____

3. **Knowledge** about how to change?

                                  1   2   3   4   5

Notes:_____

4. **Ability** to change?

                                  1   2   3   4   5

Notes:_____

5. **Reinforcement** to retain the change?

                                  1   2   3   4   5

Notes:_____

ADKAR worksheets for business change

Briefly describe the change that is being implemented at your company.

_____

_____

_____

_____

_____

_____

_____

_____

_____

_____

_____

_____

_____

_____

_____

_____

_____

_____

_____

_____

_____

_____

_____

1. Describe your *awareness* of the need to change. What are the business, customer or competitor issues that have created a need to change?

_____

_____

_____

_____

_____

_____

_____

_____

_____

_____

_____

_____

_____

_____

_____

_____

To what degree do you rate your **awareness** of the need to change?

Score

1	2	3	4	5
low				high

2. List the factors or consequences (good and bad) related to this change that affect your *desire* to change.

_____

_____

_____

_____

_____

_____

_____

_____

_____

_____

_____

_____

_____

_____

_____

_____

_____

Consider these motivating factors, including your conviction in these factors and the associated consequences, and assess your overall **desire** to change.

Score

| 1 | 2 | 3 | 4 | 5 |
| low | | | | high |

3. List the skills and *knowledge* needed to support this change.

_____

_____

_____

_____

_____

_____

_____

_____

_____

_____

_____

_____

_____

_____

_____

_____

_____

_____

Do you have a clear understanding of the change and the skills you will need to operate in the changed environment? Have you received education or training to learn these skills? To what degree do you rate your **knowledge** of the change?

Score

1	2	3	4	5
low				high

4. Considering the skills and knowledge identified in Step 3, assess your overall proficiency in each area (low, medium, high).

_____
_____
_____
_____
_____
_____
_____
_____
_____
_____
_____
_____
_____
_____
_____
_____

Review your evaluations and rate your overall **ability** to change.

Score

1   2   3   4   5

low   high

5. List the *reinforcements* that will help retain the change.
Are incentives in place to reinforce the change and make
it stick?

_____
_____
_____
_____
_____
_____
_____
_____
_____
_____
_____
_____
_____
_____

To what degree do you rate the **reinforcements** as adequate to sustain the change?

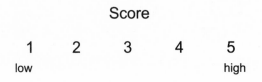

Score

1   2   3   4   5
low   high

Now transfer your scores from each worksheet to the table below. Take a moment to review your scores. Highlight the first area to score a 3 or lower. This is the starting point for addressing your personal transition through this change.

Brief description of the change:

1. **Awareness** of the need to change?   1 2 3 4 5

Notes:_____

2. **Desire** to make the change happen?   1 2 3 4 5

Notes:_____

3. **Knowledge** about how to change?   1 2 3 4 5

Notes:_____

4. **Ability** to change?   1 2 3 4 5

Notes:_____

5. **Reinforcement** to retain the change?   1 2 3 4 5

Notes:_____

Appendix C – Highlights of best practices

In your study of change management, listening to and learning from the experiences of others is a key step. This section provides questions and answers that will give you a head start. View these findings as if you are sitting across from a colleague from another company and asking questions like, "What were your greatest contributors to success?"

This chapter provides highlights of key findings from Prosci research studies involving more than 650 companies. The following responses were synthesized from hundreds of answers to these types of questions, with the most common themes and patterns prioritized in the response. The heading of each section refers to the question answered by participants. For example, the section titled "Greatest contributors to success" provides the most common answers participants gave to the question, "What were the greatest contributors to your change management project's success?"

Greatest contributors to success

Overwhelmingly, the greatest contributor to project success was effective and strong executive sponsorship. Effective sponsors:

- Are visible and accessible throughout the entire project

- Engage leaders and managers early and throughout the duration of a project

- Align priorities among organization leaders

- Directly communicate with employees and the
  project team (including change managers)
  throughout the duration of the project to build
  and maintain support for the change

Overall, the top six contributors to successful change projects were:

1. Active and visible executive sponsorship

2. Frequent and open communication about the change

   Communication messages included a clear and
   compelling reason for the change, the objectives of
   the change and the implications of not changing.
   Participants emphasized that the need for the
   change was best delivered by the sponsor or leader
   of the change.

3. Structured change management approach

   Respondents noted that the use of an established,
   easy-to-apply methodology helped increase user
   adoption. Respondents also noted that the earlier
   change management was applied, the more success
   the project achieved.

4. Dedicated change management resources and funding

   Having "change agents" across the organization and
   within organizational hierarchies ensured that
   change management was being utilized in multiple, if
   not all, functional groups across the project.

According to study respondents, it was also important to provide the appropriate amount of funding and resources required to execute the change management plans that were developed.

5. Employee engagement and participation

Activities to drive employee engagement included providing two-way communications for employees to solicit feedback; creating awareness among the end-users and front-line employees about why the change was occurring and establishing the "what's in it for me" (WIIFM) messages; and increasing involvement of employees in the decision-making process by soliciting and gathering input.

6. Support from middle management

Having the buy-in and engagement of middle management helped to ensure positive and effective communications to front-line employees. Respondents noted that ensuring that managers had adequate change management skills empowered them to be more effective leaders of change and decreased fear of power loss resulting from the change.

Greatest change management obstacles

The top obstacle to change was ineffective change management sponsorship from senior leaders. Common problems included:

- Inactive or invisible sponsors

- Poor alignment between organizational direction and the objectives of the change

- Lack of sponsor commitment to change management

- Sponsors with competing priorities or changes in sponsorship

- Sponsors at the wrong level (not high enough in the organization)

- Little or no access to the primary sponsor

- Failure to build a coalition of sponsors

Overall, the top five greatest change management obstacles were:

1. Ineffective change management sponsorship from senior leaders

2. Insufficient change management resourcing

   Participants cited a general lack of resources and funding available to conduct the necessary planning and implementation of change management.

3. Resistance to change from employees

Reasons for resistance included employees lacking understanding of why the change was needed and the "what's in it for me?", and employees being unwilling to change due to poorly handled changes in the past.

4. Middle-management resistance

Middle managers were reluctant to support the change personally or lead the change with their staff. This resistance from middle managers resulted in a lack of consistent and accurate communication about the change to their employees.

5. Poor communication

Participants cited a number of reasons that their communications were not effective, including inconsistent messages and communications not addressing the need or reason for the change.

What would you do differently on your next project?

Participants indicated that the number one thing they would do differently in the next project was get the primary sponsor on board and engaged at the start of the project.

Responses regarding the engagement of sponsors included:

- Ensuring sponsor alignment throughout the organization

- Engaging the various senior leaders that need to be on board supporting the change

- Educating and coaching sponsors

- Increasing the active and visible involvement of sponsors

- Creating a tighter connection and relationship to sponsors

Overall, the top five responses for what participants would do differently next time were:

1. Engage sponsors better

2. Start change management activities sooner

3. Emphasize employee engagement and involvement

4. Secure sufficient resources for change management

5. Improve communications

Employee resistance

Participants gave a variety of reasons for resistance by employees and managers. The top five reasons for employee resistance were:

1. Lack of awareness

Employees resisted change because they lacked awareness of why the change was being made or did not understand the nature of the change. They did not know the
business reasons for making a change or the consequences of not changing. Study participants stated that
employees resisted more when they did not have the
answer to the question "what's in it for me?" or WIIFM.
Participants also said that employees lacked awareness
because their managers were uninformed or were sending mixed messages.

Study participants stated that the most important messages to communicate to impacted employees were:

• Business reasons for the change

• Why the employees should want to participate

• Impact of the change on employees

• How the change was happening

• Details about the change

Additional key messages to employees included:

• How employees would be supported through the
  change

• To whom or where they could go for more information,
  such as training resources, updates, job aids or
  requests for additional support

- Information pertaining to how and when employees would be trained and the necessity and importance of training

2. Impact on current job role

   Many employees resisted change when they believed there would be a negative impact on their job role or workload. Specifically, employees were resistant to changes that increased their amount of work, did not allow for current process "work arounds," and would cause a loss of position or power when the change was implemented

3. Organization's past performance with change

   Participants cited the organization's past failure to implement changes as a factor in employee lack of commitment to a current change.

4. Lack of visible support and commitment from managers

   Participants cited a lack of support from employees when the employees' managers did not stress the importance of making the change or did not show a personal commitment to making the change themselves.

5. Fear of job loss

   Employees were especially fearful of any changes that could possibly affect their employment during difficult economic times.

Manager resistance

The top four reasons for manager resistance to change were:

1. Lack of awareness about and involvement in the change

   The leading reason for manager resistance to change was a lack of understanding of the scope, timeline and impact of the change on them and on their employees. Study participants stated that managers felt left out of the project planning phase, and that their expertise and proximity to the end-users was not utilized. This lack of awareness and involvement in the specifics of the project caused a lack of clarity in their roles and responsibilities in the change, and they were unsure of what was expected of them.

2. Loss of control or negative impact on job role

   Many managers felt that the change reduced the dependence on their personal knowledge and contribution, thereby making them redundant (less needed). They felt this redundancy would cause them to lose their positions of power or lose their jobs completely. If the change was not going to result in management job loss, then managers felt that the change would cause them to fail or look incompetent because it took them out of their comfort zones or changed the way they did their jobs.

3. Increased workload and lack of time

A lack of time to manage the change successfully was also a source of resistance from managers. Study participants reported that managers felt that the change itself was too cumbersome and time consuming or that they had competing priorities and had reached a point of change saturation for themselves and their employees.

4. Culture of change resistance and past failures

Another source of resistance from managers dealt with the particular culture of their organizations and the history of past change projects. Managers distrusted a particular change due to a feeling that it was "the flavor of the month" and that it would fail like past changes had failed. Another aspect of this distrust was a sense that maintaining the status quo was the safest way to prevent any of the adverse effects of a failed change.

Most common executive sponsor mistakes

Participants cited the following areas as the most common mistakes made by top-level sponsors:

- Failed to remain visible and engaged throughout the project

- Failed to demonstrate support for the project in words and actions

- Failed to effectively communicate messages about the need for change

- Ignored the people side of the change

- Delegated or abdicated the sponsorship role and responsibilities

What would project teams do differently with regard to communication?

Participants indicated that the top five changes they would make regarding their communications were:

1. More communications

   Participant responses indicated that they would communicate more, to more people, more often and to all levels within the organization. Responses also indicated that these communications should be more targeted, more face to face, more interactive and more relevant to the audience.

2. Have a communication strategy

   The second most common response reflected the need for a more detailed communication strategy, including a succinct, consistent and accurate core set of messages. A strategy would also include a more robust implementation timeline for communication activities.

3. Communicate earlier

    Participants indicated they would begin communica-
    tion earlier. These efforts included syncing to other
    communication networks, connecting to the project
    sooner and beginning in-person meetings earlier,
    even if only partial information was available.

4. More attention to senior leadership

    The fourth recommendation from participants
    involved more attention, interaction and involve-
    ment with senior leadership. Participants reported
    that they would have evoked more support and own-
    ership from senior leadership.

5. More dedicated people working on communication

    Study results revealed that communication efforts
    needed to have more people dedicated to them,
    including having more dedicated and expert
    resources assigned to producing and implementing
    communications.

About the *Best Practices in Change Management* report

The highlights in this section are compiled findings from seven change management benchmarking studies conducted by Prosci since 1998.

For more information or to obtain a copy of the most recent report, visit www.change-management.com.

Appendix D – Frequently asked questions

In most business changes, employees have questions that address the overall change and how they will be impacted. The answers to these questions are certainly unique to the business, the change and the employee. For example, answers to the question, "Why is this change necessary?" will be unique to your business conditions. However, in many cases, answers will have common themes. This appendix lists some frequently asked questions and answers adapted from the book, *Employee's Survival Guide to Change* (Hiatt). These answers may be useful as a starting point if you are faced with similar questions.

Why is change happening now?

Most changes begin outside the company many months, or even years, before internal change takes place. Research shows that most major business changes are a response to changes in the external marketplace. These external marketplace changes can result in:

- New opportunities that require immediate action

- Loss of market share (your company is losing money)

- New offers or capabilities by competitors (they're creating new business faster than your company)

- Lower prices (their cost of doing business is lower, resulting in better prices to their customers)

External business drivers take time to set in. Once they have affected the bottom line of the company, change is needed immediately. In some cases it is already too late, the internal change should have started much sooner.

What is the risk of not changing?

When external marketplace changes are reflected inside the organization, managers suddenly realize the risks of not changing.

For businesses, the risk of not changing could mean:

- Loss of jobs (even at the executive level)

- Failure in the marketplace

- Bankruptcy or loss of revenue

For employees, the risk of not changing could mean:

- Job dissatisfaction

- Fewer promotional opportunities

- Lower job security in the long term

- Immediate loss of employment

What is the rush?

We usually find out what is happening after the fact. Organizations do not always share financial information or talk about poor performance issues with employees. Therefore, when change is needed quickly, employees and even some managers may be taken by surprise. As a company we still need to react quickly to changing market conditions to remain viable. It may appear that the company is in a rush to change when actually it is already late in implementing change.

If I wait long enough, will the change just go away?

Waiting will usually not change the outcome of a change. In some cases, the company will change even in the face of resistance from employees, especially if financial success is at stake.

This does not imply that change will be bad for you. In the end many changes result in positive outcomes. Benefits might include better tools, improved work processes, more secure jobs and new opportunities.

What might the change mean to me?

Change to a business can include:

- New ways of doing work

- New systems or tools

- New reporting structures or job roles

- Shifting cultures or subcultures

- New products or services

- New markets or geographic locations

The actual change for you depends on your current job, the extent of the change, and the choices you make in response to the change.

With some changes, you may not be impacted at all. With major changes, you may be doing new work, using new tools or reporting to a new manager. With radical changes to the business, some employees may work in other departments or even move to other companies.

When the change is implemented, each person will be affected differently. In the end, how you react to the change plays an important role in how the change will impact you. In other words, what you are in control of is how you respond to change. In fact, how the organization views you and your future role in the company may depend on your response to change and the choices you make.

What are my choices?

Your choices about how to respond to change will vary as the organization moves through the change process. Think about the change in these time periods:

- When the change is first announced, but before the change is implemented

- During the change process, when the new solution is being deployed

- After the change is in place, following the implementation of the solution

Your choices and their consequences depend on which phase your organization is in. The following pages provide potential choices you may make and the likely outcomes of those choices. In some cases choices you make may have negative outcomes. They may be bad for you and for the organization. Other choices you make will benefit you and enhance your ability to thrive in a changing organization.

The choices shown on the following pages are separated into:

- Choices with typically *negative* outcomes

- Choices with typically *positive* outcomes

These examples help illustrate the conscious and unconscious decisions we all make regarding change.

Choices when the change is first announced

Choices that typically have a *negative* outcome when the change is first announced:

- Talk badly about the proposed change with your peers or subordinates

- Talk negatively about the organization or people in the organization

- Talk one way in public, but say otherwise in private conversations

- Stop performing your current tasks or perform them carelessly

- Have secret meetings with your subordinates where the change is minimized or not taken seriously

Choices that typically have a *positive* outcome when the change is first announced:

- Learn about the change

- Ask how you can help

- Find out how you can prepare for the change

- Display a positive outlook

- Encourage constructive conversations with fellow employees

- Be open and honest with your feedback about the change

- Be quiet and curious (this choice is acceptable during the early phases of a change)

Choices during the change transition

Choices that typically have a *negative* outcome during the transition to the new solution:

- Block progress or sabotage the change process

- Talk negatively about the change in private conversations

- Ignore the change, pretend that it is not happening (denial)

- Prevent others from participating in the design of the solution or implementation of the design

Choices that typically have a *positive* outcome during the transition to the new solution:

- Ask questions about the future

- Ask how the change will impact day-to-day operations

- Provide input to the solution

- Find out what new skills and abilities you will need to perform effectively after the change is in place

- Assess your own strengths and weaknesses

- Identify training that will be available to fill skill gaps

- Take advantage of the change to develop new skills and grow professionally

- Begin to "let go" of the status quo

Choices after the change is implemented

Choices that typically have a *negative* outcome after the change is implemented:

- Avoid using the new work processes or tools whenever possible

- Tell peers or subordinates that using the new work processes or tools is not a big deal and shouldn't be taken too seriously

- Talk negatively about the organization with customers

- Revert to the old way of doing work when problems or issues arise with the change

- Take advantage of problems during implementation to argue why the change will never work

- Complain about the decision to make the change

Choices that typically have a *positive* outcome after the change is implemented:

- Reinforce the change with peers and subordinates

- Help the business achieve the objectives of the change (be results oriented)

- Avoid reverting back to old processes or ways of doing work when problems arise with the new processes and systems; be patient

- Help solve problems that arise with new work processes and tools

What are the consequences of not changing?

The consequences to you of not changing depend on how critical the change is to the business and your role. For changes that are less critical to business success or that do not directly impact you, the consequences may be minimal. However, if you elect not to support the change, and the change is critical to the success of the organization, the possible consequences are:

- Loss of employment

- Reassignment or transfer with the potential for lower pay

- Lost opportunities for promotion or advancement in the organization

- Reduced job satisfaction as you fight the organization and the organization fights you

What are the benefits of supporting the change?

The benefits of supporting the change, especially a change that is critical to the success of the organization, include:

- Enhanced respect and reputation within the organization

- Improved growth opportunities (especially for active supporters of the change)

- Increased job satisfaction (knowing you are helping your organization respond effectively to a rapidly changing marketplace)

- Improved job security

What if I disagree with the change or I feel they are fixing the wrong problem?

Be patient. Keep an open mind. Make sure you understand the business reasons for the change. However, don't be afraid to voice your specific objections or concerns. If your objections are valid, chances are good they will come to light and be resolved. If you feel strongly against a specific element of the change, let the right people know and do it in an appropriate manner.

What if they've tried before and failed?

The history of your company may include some previous change projects that failed. If failure is what employees are accustomed to, the organization will have a hard time erasing the past. In order for companies to be successful, everyone must be prepared to accept the past as history and focus on what lies ahead.

What if I am forced to do more for the same pay?

When your organization is undergoing a change, this usually means that new processes, systems or skills are required. Your role in the changed environment may include learning these new processes or acquiring new skills. Indeed, some of your responsibilities may change. For the old way of doing things, compensation may actually decrease as the value of that work to the organization goes down. However, compensation for new work may increase as the value for new services and products increases. This is a part of change.

About the authors

Jeff Hiatt is the founder of the Change Management Learning Center (www.change-management.com) and CEO of Prosci. Jeff is the author of *The Perfect Change, Employee's Survival Guide to Change, ADKAR: a model for change in business, government and our community*, and co-author of *Winning with Quality*. Jeff has led research projects with more than 2600 companies on change management and business process design.

Tim Creasey is the Chief Development Officer of Prosci, leading research efforts and guiding product and service development. He serves as managing editor and contributor for the Change Management Learning Center and has written hundreds of change management tutorials. Tim is a frequent conference speaker and is the lead facilitator for Prosci's well-known change management webinar series.